Jackie

Her Words
and
Words About Her

Edited by
Trina Spain Flynn
and
George Spain

Ideas into Books®
WESTVIEW
Kingston Springs, Tennessee

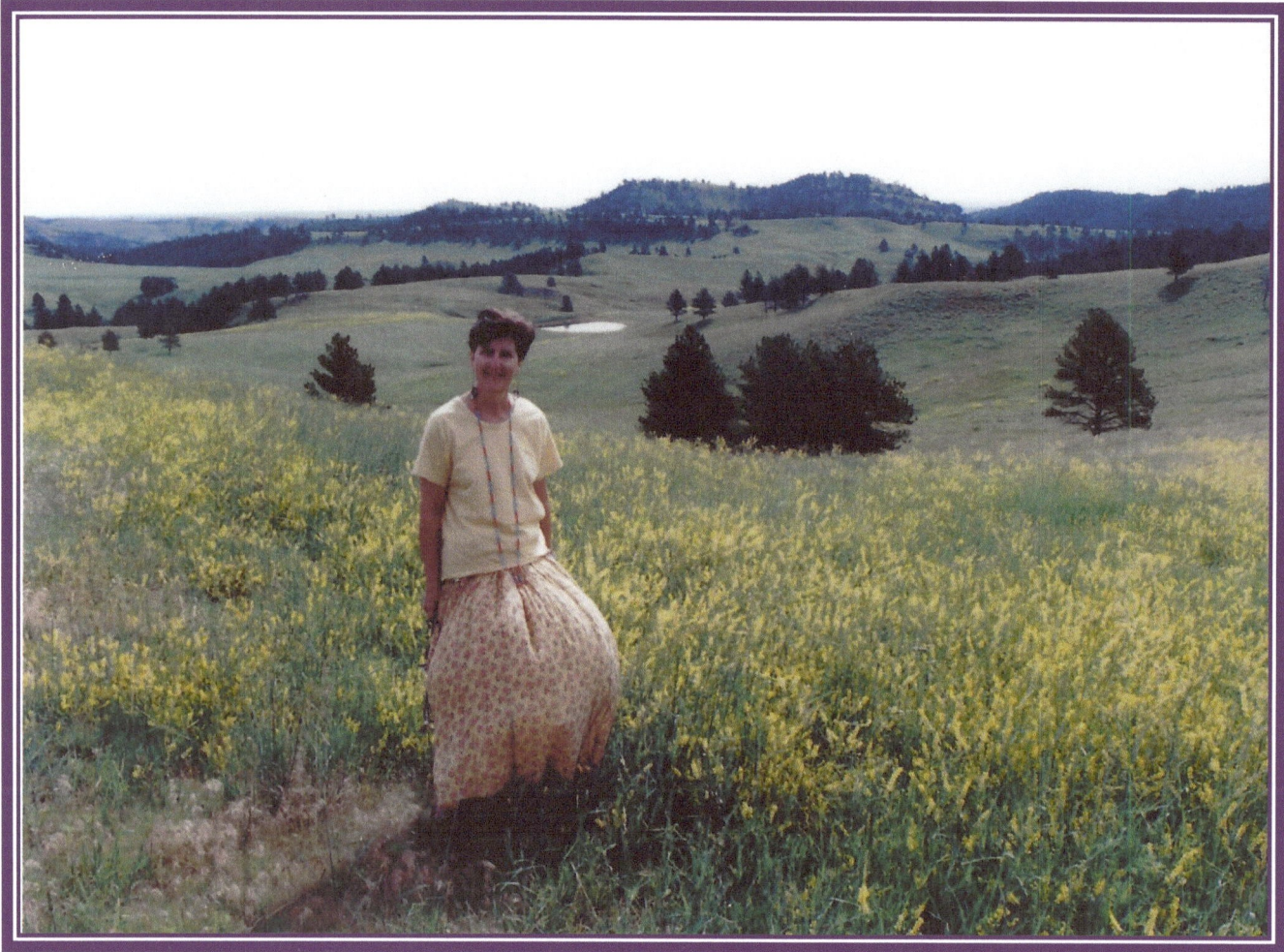

Dedicated to

Jacqulyn "Jackie" Katrine Burton Spain

Brad, Lynch, Trina, Adam, and Darwin, Our Children

Our Thirteen Grandchildren and Five Great Grandchildren

Our Dear Friends and All Who Loved Jackie

My "Precious," My "Babes," My "Jackie"
There's No One Like Her.

George Spain

GENEALOGICAL

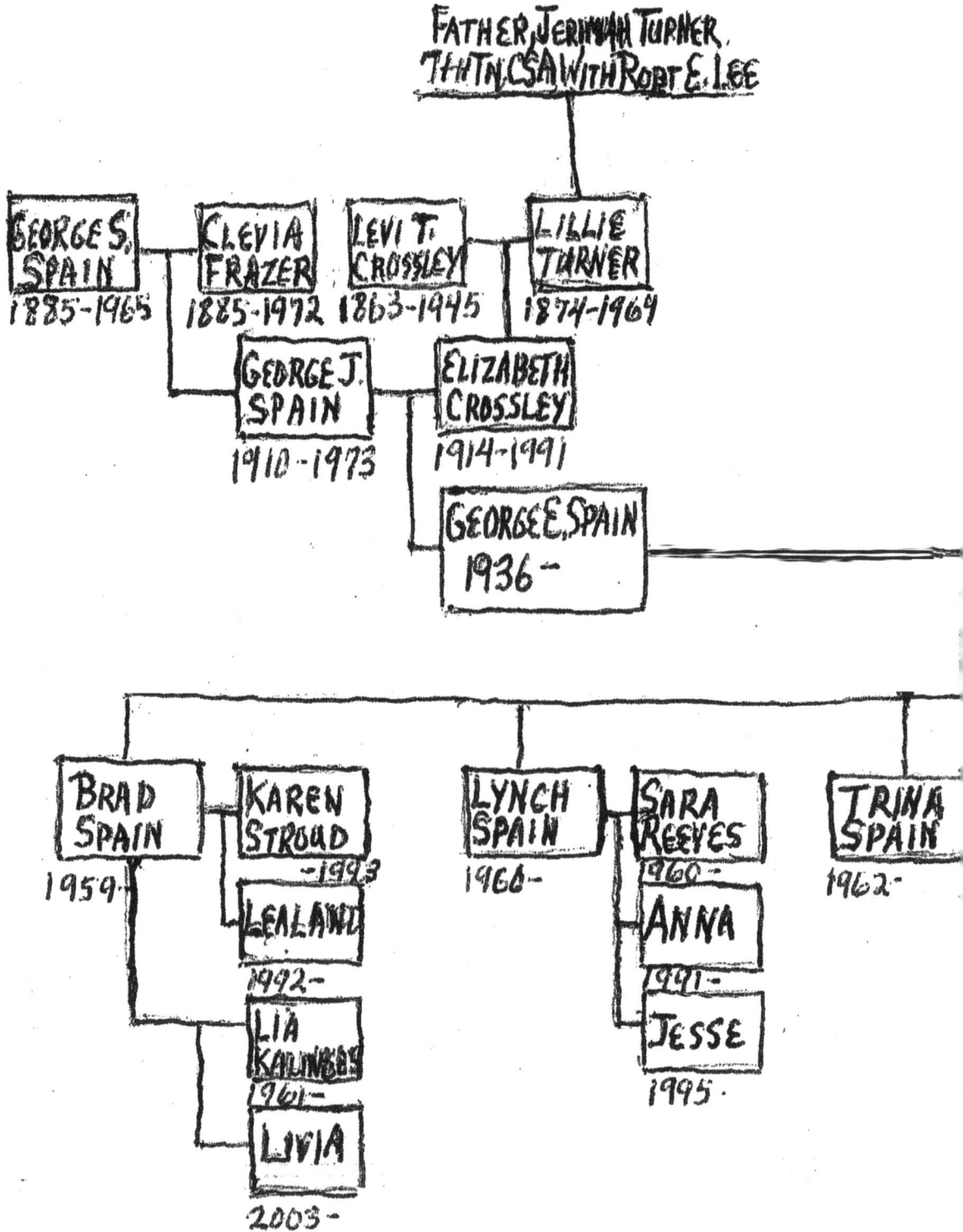

FATHER JERIMIAH TURNER,
7TH TN CSA WITH ROBT E. LEE

GEORGE S. SPAIN
1885-1965

CLEVIA FRAZER
1885-1972

LEVI T. CROSSLEY
1863-1945

LILLIE TURNER
1874-1969

GEORGE J. SPAIN
1910-1973

ELIZABETH CROSSLEY
1914-1991

GEORGE E. SPAIN
1936-

BRAD SPAIN
1959-

KAREN STROUD
-1993

LEALAND
1992-

LIA KALUNBOS
1961-

LIVIA
2003-

LYNCH SPAIN
1960-

SARA REEVES
1960-

ANNA
1991-

JESSE
1995-

TRINA SPAIN
1962-

2

TABLE

FATHER, WILLIAM PEARSON
1st Tn. CSA Bro. Killed Kennsaw Mtn.

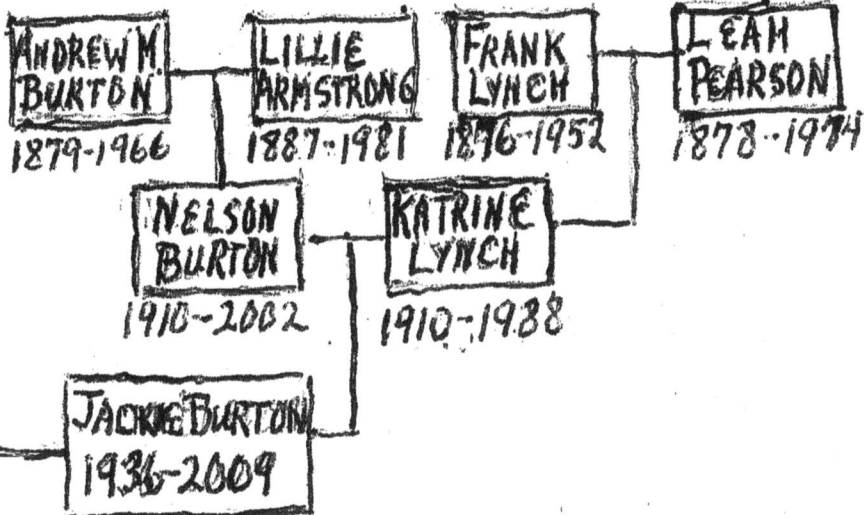

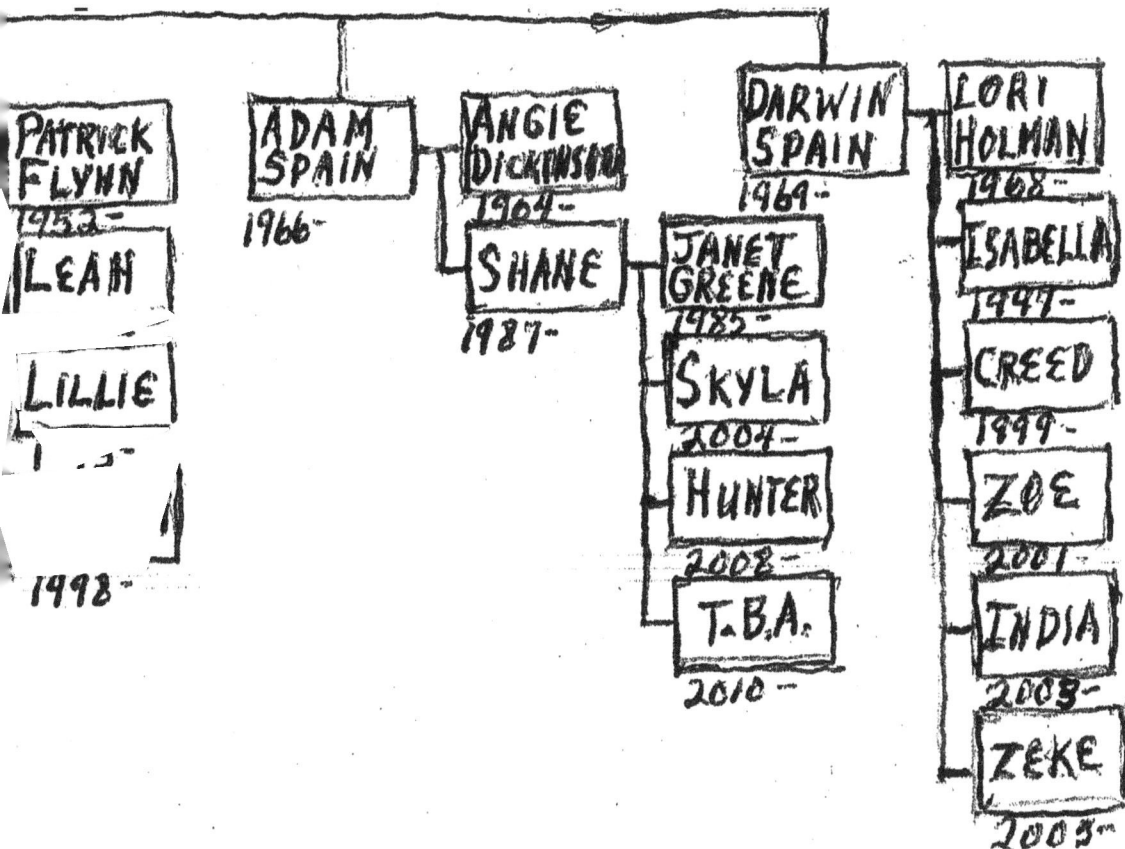

ANDREW M BURTON 1879-1966	LILLIE ARMSTRONG 1887-1981	FRANK LYNCH 1876-1952	LEAH PEARSON 1878-1974

NELSON BURTON 1910-2002

KATRINE LYNCH 1910-1988

JACKIE BURTON 1936-2009

PATRICK FLYNN 1952-

LEAH

LILLIE

1998-

ADAM SPAIN 1966-

ANGIE DICKINSON 1964-

SHANE 1987-

DARWIN SPAIN 1969-

LORI HOLMAN 1968-

JANET GREENE 1985-

SKYLA 2004-

HUNTER 2008-

T.B.A. 2010-

ISABELLA 1997-

CREED 1999-

ZOE 2001-

INDIA 2003-

ZEKE 2005-

HUSBAND'S NAME _George Edward Lynch_

When Born _Oct. 5, 1936_ Where _N___

Christened _____ Where _____

When Died _____ Where _____

When Buried _____ Where _____

When Married _June 22, 1956_ Where _N_

Other Wives (if any)
Number (1) (2) etc. _____

His Father _George Joseph_ His Mother's

WIFE'S MAIDEN NAME _Jacqulyn Katrine_

When Born _Jan 12, 1936_ Where _N_

Christened _____ Where _____

When Died _____ Where _____

When Buried _____ Where _____

Other Husb. (if any)
Number (1) (2) etc. _____

Her Father _Nelson Burton_ Her Mother's Ma

Male or Female	CHILDREN (Arrange in order of birth)	WHEN BORN		
		Day	Month	Year
M	1	Nov	14	195
M	2 Thomas Lynch	July	19	196
F	3 Elizabeth Katrine	June	23	196
M	4 Carla	ag 30		1966
M		ay 14		196
	12			

nily Group Sheet, Form F2
The Everton Publishers, 526 North Main Street, Logan, Utah
burial date is known on children and not death date, write
ial date, prefix (Bur). Use reverse side for additional info.

4

shville, Tenn

_____ (Husband's Full Name)

hville, Tenn.

Name _Flaane Elizabeth Crossley,_

urton

shville, Tenn.

_____ Date _____

_____ Compiler _____

Address _____

n Name _Dice Leah Katrine Lynch_ State _____

WHERE BORN Town or Place	County	State or Country	WHEN DIED Day	Month	Year	Married
Nash David Jr.						Date April 23 1983 To Kristina Patterte
"	"	"				Date Dec. 10, 1983 To Sara Lee Reeves
"	"	"				Date May 16 1987 To Patrick Harden Flynn
"	"	"				Date Dec. 20, 1988 To Angela Dickinson
"	"	"				Date To
						Date To
						Date To
						Date To
						Date To
						Date To
						Date To
						Date To
						Date To
						Date To
						Date To

Mr. and Mrs. Nelson Burton
request the honour of your presence
at the marriage of their daughter
Jacqulyn Katrine
to
Mr. George Edward Spain
Friday, the twenty-second of June
Nineteen hundred and fifty-six
at eight o'clock in the evening
daylight saving time
in the garden at Seven Hills
Hillsboro Road
Nashville, Tennessee

MARRIAGE CERTIFICATE

THIS IS TO CERTIFY THAT THE

Rite of Matrimony

Between _George E. Spain_ Age _19_

and _Zacqulyn K. Burton_ Age _20_

was solemnized by _Mac W. Craig_

on _22_ day of _June_ _1956_, as
the same appears of record in the office of the Clerk of the County
Court of the aforesaid County at Nashville, Tennessee.
WITNESS my hand and seal of the said Court, at office, this
the _11_ day of _June_ 19_58_.

JnoBClabb
Clerk of the Davidson County Court.

George Rooker
Deputy Clerk

BOOK _78_ PAGE _96_ NO. _30381_

I don't know if I've shared this memory or not.

One day, Jackie brought her wedding dress to the dorm for all the girls in Sewall (or was it Sewell) Hall to ooh and aah over!

It was soooo beautiful and distinctively Jackie.

I noticed two things about it right off and remember them to this day because they were unusual for that day and time.

First, it was not white. It was a pale, dusty rose color.

Second, it had short sleeves. When she said the wedding was being held outside, I thought that choice such a sensible one.

Later on, Jackie Kennedy wore a short sleeved gown and I think her wedding was outside, too (not sure), and, since then, many old ideas about weddings have changed.

Only white flowers in the church, only white wrapping on wedding gifts, everything white, white, white.

Our wedding took place in early September in sweltering heat-- inside--and my white, long-sleeved dress got soaking wet with sweat. Could only imagine what it was like for Harry with double long sleeves.

Looking back, I'm so happy to have those memories of Jackie's wedding dress, reflecting her exquisite taste and her penchant for breaking the mold in favor of sensible and practical considerations.

Hope my memories are accurate!

Sometimes I do as Emily Dickinson   advised "Tell the truth, but tell it slant."

Maxine

Sent from my iPhone

Maxine Rose

8

Her Words

Dear George,

I've told you a million times how sweet and handsome and wonderful and gorgeous you are. Really, I've never met anyone that I enjoy being with any more - we really have a big time together 'cause we're both so nutty. I'll never forget Florida as long as I live - I hope we can go again next year. I'm looking forward to a great summer - if you'll come to see me for about a week. Daddy would get a kick out of that too! I want to get you on the skis — wow!!- watch out!! I wish you all would happen to drive by the lake Saturday. Love to have ya. I'll miss seeing you everyday this summer — take care of your muscles - I'd hate for anything to happen to them after all your hard work.

Love ya loads,

Jackie

written in my
1955 Lipscomb
Backlog
George

Written in our Wedding Book by Jackie, not long after our marriage June 22, 1956.
— George Spain
2009

How We Met

When I came to Lipscomb I met George. The first time I remember seeing him was on the side steps of Sewell Hall. I really thought he was a "tough cat" with his "flat top" and blue sweat shirt & jeans!

My freshman year we were the closest of friends. I went with Nicky Boone and he and George were best friends. We were together most of the time though. That summer George came to see me — in September he went to Memphis with us. We saw "Marty." I said "George why don't I just marry you and solve all my problems!" On the way back to Estill Springs our romance started. He went home on Saturday and I went to Nashville Monday for dinner and a show and he came home with me that night. He told me he loved me and we started going steady September 13th, 1955. That same day. He stayed a week & we both went back to school the 20th

In February we decided to get married. George was going to talk to Mama & Daddy the night of the Globe Trotter game (around the 18th). Mrs. Spain thought we had already spoken to them so at the game she spilled the beans. We could see them talking and I knew what had happened. After the game we did talk to them, and they seemed quite pleased. "Whatever will make you happy, will make us happy." George was petrified, but it turned out fine!

His mother gave me her ring. We took it to the jewelry store Saturday to get a mounting for it. On Monday George picked it up and at about 1:00 or 2:00 P.M. in the after on February 22nd, 1956, he presented me with a beautiful engagement ring. Of course I knew about it, so he "tortured" me before he gave it to me. That night at supper everybody wanted to see it. We really were thrilled. I still gaze at it!

Our Engagement

Sat. May 25 1968

Dear Mama & Daddy,

I know you have had mass con-
fusion at your house these past two
weeks and I do hope the house
cleaning went off to your satisfaction
Was this the week end for your
big high school party? Good luck!

I felt very honored that you
came on Mother's Day and we missed Daddy. I know it was an effort
for you and I really did appreciate
your coming and then your note.

I've been very busy too, but
with a little pleasure thrown in
this week. Mrs. Edom took me to the
Centenial Club for a coffee and beautiful exhibit on table arrangements,
which was out of this world! This
was Wed. and Fri. Adam and I had to
leave home at 9:30, go to Lynch's circus,

eat lunch with Irina and have a private
birthday party, since hers doesn't come
within the school year. We spent about
two hours with Mimi then and she
gave me the twin picture frame with
the picture of Daddy and the other of
3, L, and Daddy. She was there all by
herself and it seemed real pitiful, but
we had a nice visit. She said she had
laid these pictures aside for me and I
cleaned them up today and am so
happy to have them.

Tracy G. was up early getting
all his work done, grass cut and pool cleaned,
pony ridden and swimming. I had
work inside of course, while Adam
took a nap. He took the others to
Water Valley for fishing & picnic and now
Adam is up, had his lunch and it's
our turn at the pool.

Next week is our last full week of
school, but will be packed full with
picnics, achievement tests, conferences
and parties.

Irina's class is going to Eagleville
to a farm Tues., Lynn's class is coming

here on Thursday and Brad's class may come the following week where they go only half a day til Wed. I'm must say I'll be relieved when all this going has slowed down some.

We are still looking forward to your group coming, but I couldn't remember if you said the 1st or the 8th? We were going to have our teachers out sometime too and needed to get these dates straight. But we can have them on any day; I just didn't want to make a mistake.

Adam is beginning to get more sun now and may fool us with his tan. He is nearly always asleep during the hot part of the day so really hasn't had a good go at the sun! For his birth-day he needs a molded plastic pool (not blow up) to play in and a tricycle

I don't mean to sound like you have an ultimateum, but just making suggestions. We don't need any clothes if you don't plan to get either of these let me know and I'll see about it.

It's really hot out here — I need to jump in and cool off, then start on a letter to Jane. I haven't written her in months, along with everyone else I know who lives away.

Hope your parties are successful and we looking forward to seeing all of you in June.

Much love,
Jackie

I need to send Mike's baby a gift — I guess she is still very small?

After leaving FCHS in 1954, I took a trip out west with my parents to visit my aunt in California and came home to have the most glorious summer. I was on the lake with Jane and Parker Smith almost every day, but finally had to pack up and go to college and try to act like a partial grownup.

I went to David Lipscomb College and graduated there in 1958 with one summer school thrown in. But I'm getting ahead of myself. I met George Spain the very first day at DL as I was moving in, and we became good friends right away, but I dated his best friend! Later George and I started dating and fell in love and got married in 1956.

He had one year of college left and I had two. We did finish, but as I was receiving my diploma, I had the first pangs of morning sickness. Timed it just right! Brad was born in January of '59, Lynch in '60, Trina in '62, Adam in '66, and Darwin in '69.

We moved to the country in Williamson Co. after Trina was born and played farmer for about 20 years. It was a very special time for our family. We had cows, horses, chickens, goats, pigs and of course dogs. I'm afraid the dogs ate the cats! We always had a big garden, but most importantly there were plenty of chores to go around. I think they all learned how to work and appreciate nature.

We would have stayed there forever, but circumstances forced us to make a change, so we came back to Nashville and have been here on North Observatory Dr. ever since.

All our children have married and we have an even dozen grandchildren. They range from age 17 to 8 months. All but one family lives in Davidson and Williamson Co. and one lives in Cleveland, TN.

My parents have both died, Mother in '89 and Daddy in 2002 at the age of 92. He stayed in Estill Springs until 2001 when he came to Nashville to assisted living, still driving!!!!

After his death, George and I renovated the house in Estill and enjoy relaxing there a few days a week when possible, watching the Great Blue Herons, geese and other birds and animals. It is a great place for the grandchildren to come and play with Baba and Papa, swimming and canoeing and enjoying being cousins together.

The nice thing about coming home is renewing old friendships and reminiscing about the lazy hazy days of youth.

I came to FCHS from Memphis in the 10th grade and I'm so thankful for the years with you that were really so special to me. Even though I was an outsider you welcomed me in and made me feel apart of community of old friends. The atmosphere was so much more wholesome; the 50's were truly a unique time. I felt so blessed to be in Franklin Co.

HOW TO CELEBRATE YOUR BIRTHDAY IF YOU'RE OVER 29...

...QUIETLY

With much love
George, Jackie & Children

(I didn't really forget,
I'm just slow about doing
what I plan; gathering
together film, people, animals + a pretty day.) We're
got everybody here doing
"his thing" and doing it
very well I might add.
Brad's hawk is flying
across the field free now.
Nina loves Obu and lives
for the weekend to ride,
also she gets about 20 eggs
a day from her chickens and
sells several dozen a week.
Adam is doing so well riding
too. Lynel worked with him
every day for weeks.

As you see Lassie had pups
again — 10 this time, but one
passed.
Brad is going to Washington
D.C. with a student group
during spring vacation (if his
grades have come up!).
We sent the pigs to be pro-
cessed this week and they
should be ready Friday. If
we make a good garden and
kill the steer our fell our grocery bill should go down some.
Our fryers are real good too, but
all that feed sure was high.
Darren had a flu virus for
a week and then an ear in-
fection, but he is feeling much
better now.
It is getting so pretty outside
but always alot to do in the
yard — if I could get some work
Brad is going to work with
Heavy Well Drilling Co. this summer and Lynet might go to a
stable.
I'm hoping to take a couple
of short courses this spring — something to get out.
I hope your fire business
has been working out alright
with insurance etc. I know it
is a terrible ordeal. If it isn't
too much trouble we would
like to come spend the day
during their vacation. I'll let
you know.

Love again,
Jackie

22

The past year, starting with December of '86, had been exciting, busy, precious, and traumatic; Never a dull moment in the Spain household.

In Dec. 1986, our Marine son, Adam, came home from England with a delightful and lively young lady to marry. They said, "Mama you plan the wedding." But as mothers sometimes do, I got a little carried away and this intimate affair exploded into something a little bigger than first conceived. We were able to have a reception at home, though, and it was very nice and a lot of fun.

After Xmas, we settled back into our regular routine, but not for long — Time to get ready for another wedding. Irina announced that she was getting married in May. Pat Flynn is a musician, who plays guitar in a country music band called "New Grass Revival." Irina met Pat in '85, I think, and it was immediate love. Their weddin plans were very simple, but again Mama got excited. Their guest list was limited to family and only a few friends. We had the wedding at home in the yard and it was a beautiful day and a very special occasion.

At this time my mother Trixie was sick again with more 'bladder' surgery. She was in the hospital and unable to come to Trina's wedding. After her second round of Chemo-therapy & numerous investigations into the bladder, she is ~~now~~ very weak and in poor condition. She is now considering surgery to have the bladder removed. It is so difficult for her and sad for us to see such an exceedingly beautiful and strong mother, become so feeble — she is still beautiful. We are praying for a peaceful resolution for her, whatever she chooses to do.

After our May wedding, we ~~recuperated~~ several the summer and

then come Aug. 13, 1987 and a precious thing happened. Shane Micheal
Spain was born to Angie & Adam
Spain in Jacksonville, No. Carolina.
This grandmother rushed immediately to the scene to help the new
little family when they came home
from the hospital. I stayed for
two weeks and relished every moment
George, Trina, and Darwin drove
over from Nashville to take me
home, but I'm afraid that all our
hearts' had been captured by Shane
Micheal. I just regret that his
grandmother and grandfather in England have not seen him in person
yet and have not been able to share
these stages of growth that go so
quickly.

We had two graduations last
spring. Our baby son, Darwin, graduated from David Lipscomb High School
and is now a freshman in that same
college. Brad's (our oldest) wife, Trina,
graduated from DLC, magna cum

she is now a social worker at Williamson
County Human Services. Brad has his
own landscaping business and seems
to be doing very well.

In September our second son,
Lynch, was in a bad car accident
and broke his neck. For several days
he lay totally immobile and in
severe pain, in traction waiting to
see if his neck bones would pull
back into place with out having to
have surgery. Knowing that he
could die or be permanently paralized,
made these days very stressful
and prayful. But praise God, these
things didn't happen and he was
put in a "halo", which is an ap-
paratus that screws into the scull
and is attached to a rigid vest —
this allows one to be mobile without moving the neck. He wore this
for three months and just before
Xmas it was taken off. The whole
process is very discomforting, but
thank God for this medievil looking
cure. Lynch is doing well now. It's

been a life altering experience for him. This spring he is going to go back to college — UTC — and perhaps become a teacher. His wife Sara teaches second grade at a private school in Nashville.

When Lynch got hurt, Adam was able to get an emergency leave and they all came home. So we were able to spoil Shane Micheal a little more, although most of my days were taken up caring for my "big baby".

This same week Mama went back to the hospital. It's too bad they couldn't have both been in the same one!

In November George and I went to New York with two other couples. We had some whirlwind fun, took in three plays, and ate and walked alot. We are hoping to go back this fall — save those pennies.

We had a wonderful Xmas, with all our children home and well. I think I fed dozens of people for days.

It was like a full service cafeteria; Serve yourself and by all means clean up yourself.

It was a wonderful time, and we enjoyed an extended visit with Angie and the baby, after Adam had to go back to N.C.. Now Adam is on a six month float in the Mediterranean, compliments of "Uncle Sam". We are praying for a safe return home. (Do you get the idea that I spend alot of time on my knees?)

This spring Brian will also be going back to school full time for a Masters degree in psychology. For the past few weeks she has been enjoying some free time from work and time with Pat before he goes back on the road.

I guess that just about covers the major events of the past year. Hasn't it been interesting? George and I are surviving rather well; although we are hoping for a little less excitement in the coming year. Of course we would accept the joy that more babies would bring, and that's always a possibility.

Writing this little synopsis of our year has been on my mind for some time now, but I was too busy before Xmas. We have several friends around the country and world that we think about often, but just don't take the time to correspond with. I hope this will make-up for my lack of attention.

George and I hope you are all being blessed daily, as we have been.

Written by Jackie

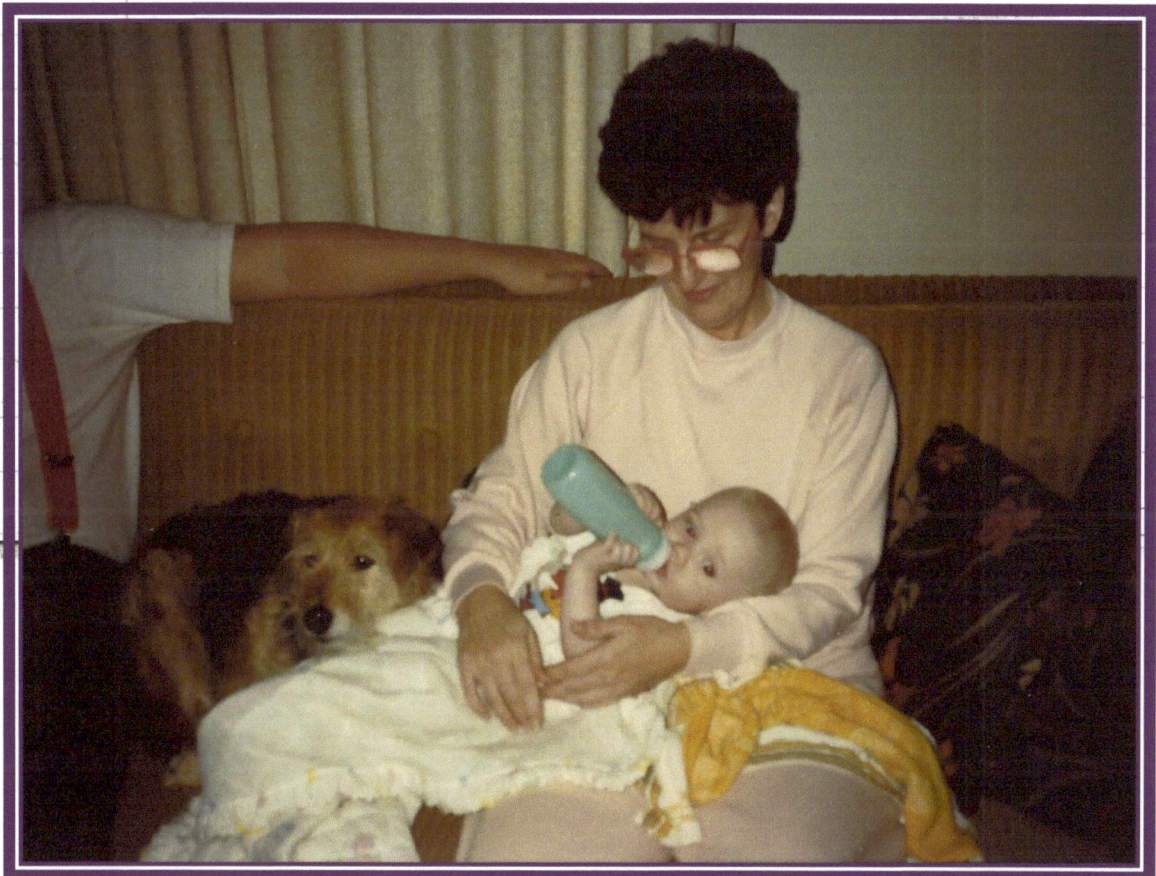

31

My dearest love,

My plan was to write a love message for you to read daily, but I found myself wandering in and out of years and events until I was overwhelmed with thoughts of you, not knowing how to put down in words all of these feelings. And then I thought, although everything that has preceded this day is certainly meaningful, in that we have come to this day together, it is only this day that is of greatest value because we are together loving deeper.

I am thankful for all the days that brought us to this point of loving. Nothing matters to me as much as you do and how you feel toward me. I know that you love me.

I'll be so far away, in distance, that a week will seem like forever. I'll miss you and wish you could be with me.

I love you so much, it hurts

Jackie

12-14-89

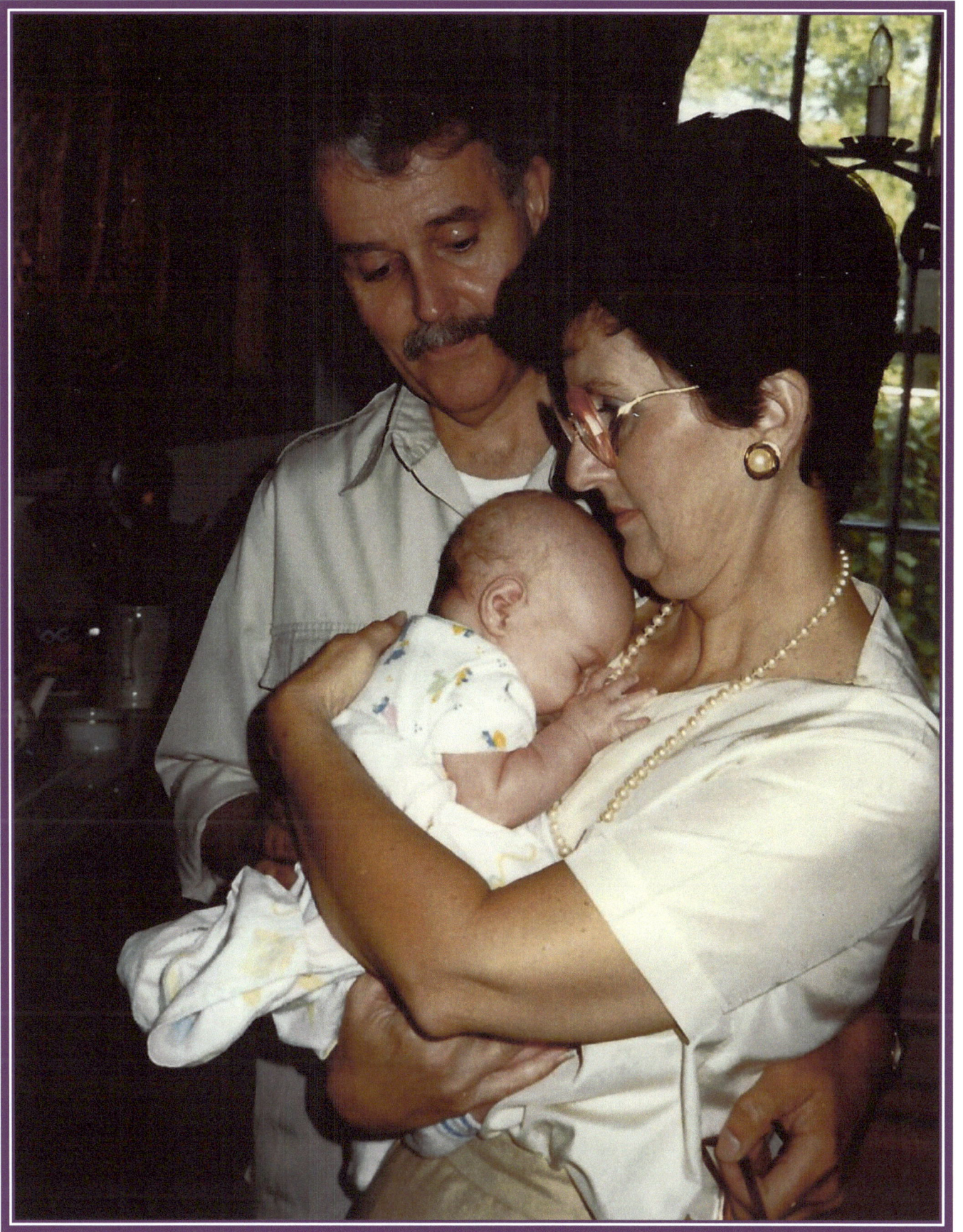

Dear loved ones,

Here we are into the New Year and I'm just getting to our Xmas greeting. We had some other more pressing activities to attend to. We discovered the second week in Nov. That my cancer had come back in my lumber spine and a place in my mid back between my lung and spine. I immediately had 10 RT and straight into Chemo Dec. 18th, 19th, and 20th. I got really sick and went to the hospital for 1 ½ days and home Xmas Eve. We had a great day Xmas; the girls took care food and all, while I sat and watched. Must say, it was pretty neet! I go back for three more Chemo treatments Jan. 15th ,16th , and17th. The 18th I have a shot of Nuelasta which is supposed to give you flu like symptoms. My hair will not be falling out as I first thought, because the meds were changed to one that does not cause that.

Up until that time we had a fun year: going to Estill whenever possible and taking kids in the summer to play. Sally, our Lab loves the lake too, but the nesting geese go crazy when she goes in the water. They come and swim all around her honking and honking!

 Adam came home from Afghanistan in the spring and worked for us in Estill redoing the patio. It looks so much better and will last another 50 years, I'm sure. Brad and his men built us a beautiful rail fence across the front and a wire fence along the side to redefine our property line. Now the corn field won't keep creeping over into our yard! Trinie and Dandy's ole pear tree is producing great crops, since it had a major pruning a couple of years ago. So I am freezing and preserving lot of pears and giving away a lot. Before we got fenced in, someone came and picked every pear, all the way to the top!!!

Every year in the fall our whole family goes to Pickett State Park near Jamestown, TN to hike and play and ride horses. This year our youngest rider was five yr. old., Zoe. We've been going for about 13 yrs. Shane was just about six and now he is ready to go to Marine boot camp, Jan. 15th.
Pray for Shane's well being.

This year Adam, Angie, and Shane, Lynch, Sara, Anna, and Jesse were missing from our group picture.

George is about to finish the 1st rewrite on his book. Of course, I have taken up so much of his time lately. He is such a loving and conscientious nurse, ready to serve in any way he can. I don't know what I would do without his support and care.

All our kids are doing fine. We are still holding at 13 grandchildren. Brad has a boy and a girl, Lynch and Sara have two girls, Trina and Pat have two girls and a boy, Adam and Angie have the oldest "man", and Darwin and Lori have three girls and two boys. They are all wonderful people and we are so proud of each of them.

Next year, hopefully we will have a better report. Please keep us in your prayers. Much love to all, Jackie and George

Thursday, Oct. 18, 2007

My dearest children and grandchildren,

If I wake up in the night and can't gp back to sleep, I compose the most beautiful thoughts and letters to each of you in my mind, and then when I wake up I can't remember what I said or how I said it. But believe me, it was great!!!

I don't want to seem morbid at this time, as I'm waiting for surgery next Wed., but I thought what a wonderful opportunity, while I have time and a relatively sound mind to tell you all some of the things that are on my heart. This may not be organized and well put together, but more like a stream of consciousness.

My plan is to right this general letter to all and then a personal note to each of you. Some of you have had longer to make memories with me, but my prayer is that I will live long enough for there to be a memory. In any case, whether the memories are long or short or non-existant, know that I love each one of my babies so much (I mean my in-law babies as well). You are what makes life so wonderful and meaningful, to have left a part of oneself to carry on the love of God and family. You all have been so blessed with a long string of fine ancestors from every side that can give you a sense of "being somebody", but most of all, you have built your own lives and characters into something that can stand on its own and never be ashamed among men.

There are so many stories and times that we have experienced with our children and I could make a list a mile long of great snakey stories, hawk tales, horse rides, milking stories and snakes, hikes, fires, temporarily lost babies, pool days and snakes, snow and ice days, catching fairies and the fairy rock, creek stories, animal births, human births, parties, so many happy days and some scarey days, chain saw massacre movies, trips and into the present times, Pickett, Jams, wild Xmases and cousins. The most fun is to sit and listen to stories being told and how many times a day I spanked everybody! Make your parents take the time to tell you real stories about their childhood and adventures.

My own childhood seems rather bland compared to our children, but I do remember some pretty big events like WW11 and the days of rationing stamps and meat tokens and not having roller skates or new shoes or cars or tires. We were always going fishing or hunting and we always had a flat tire. It seemed like it was always raining when it happened..I was at Mother and Father Lynch's when the war was over. Ben and I were playing in the gravel in the driveway far from the house and Father Lynch starting shooting his pistol off on the porch. People shouted and sang and danced in the streets all night as the court house bell tolled on.

I remember my first day at FCHS, my first day at DLC, the first time I saw George, our first date, of course our wedding, and then babies, and so that brings us full circle.

I am so blessed to have seen our children grow into such fine adults, with so many kind, wise , good and fun characteristics and talents. It is impossible for me to express what each of you means to me. You are each so very different and at the same time, very much alike. The thing I have been most proud about is that you all care for each other. You have always loved and respected us, even when we didn't do the right thing and made mistakes as parents. .Just know that we tried to do out best and hope that you can build on what we did and be better and better parents. I see that you all know much more than I did.

I am so proud of my in-law children as well and love you so much. You are like my own and feel so blessed to have shared the bond that I feel is there.

CHRISTMAS JAM 2005

SATURDAY, DECEMBER 3

7:00 P.M. - ON

THE GEORGE SPAIN HOUSE

1724 N. OBSERVATORY DRIVE

NASHVILLE, TN

PLEASE BRING FINGER FOOD

(no alcohol)

ARRIVAL

Reset a/c or heat (74 or 75 is comfortable)

Be sure you unlock the door knobs , so you want lock yourself
out
If you do get locked out there is a key under the turquoise brick
under the tools outside

Linens for twin beds are in the living room closet
Linens for sofa bed are the master closet

Ice maker works, but dispenser doesn't, get ice out by hand
Dishwasher has been programed, just press start

Boat keys are in top drawer to left of frig
Lock boats as you found them
Must wear life jacket (in basement)

RULES FOR CHILDREN
Don't take new towels to lake (old towels in laundry room)
CHILDREN DON'T EAT ALL OVER HOUSE
Don't come in wet
Don't leave wet things on furniture or floors
Don't jump on furniture and beds

There is a grill and charcoal in the new shed on house
There is a bad mitten set there also

Estill rules

DEPARTURE

Reset a/c to 77 and heat to 60

Close and lock master bath windows

Hook porch screens

Put dirty sheets and towels in laundry room (not duvet covers) do not wash

 PORCH fans off, cover daybed with spread, cover lamp with yellow fabric, bring cushions inside, fold tablecloth over with wrong side out

Run disposal and flush toilets again (put a little vinegar in kitchen drains)

Empty trash and lock in cans
Weekenders, put cans at roadside for Monday pick-up

Wash dishes if there are any, but do not leave running appliances unattended

CHECK YOUR LOCK UP ONE MORE TIME
Leave key in designated hiding place (lock dead bolt first, jiggling door a bit, then lock the door knob)

Water plants (thanks)
Be sure the hoses are off and empty

46 yrs.

comments

First time I saw Jim — lookin like James
Dean — flat top & duck tails — muscles how much
weight did
Good friends in college Fr. the you gain
first date — dove hunt Soph. summin

Married '56

Dolly — shot gun

Sweet little fat "George Edward" Ron

married '56

finished college

puppies?

worked Cain Sloan

Welfare Dept. $250 per mo.

Anna belle Clement helped
School of Social Work

Vanderbilt

people there influencial
Columbia

Everybody bailed out Geo. + a
Secretary

You know how wimpy — I think Geo
word Mental Health Ser. (as we know it
etc.)

George's Retirement

cooking skills incredible
coffee in bed
classic weenies
peanut butter & jelly – Sunday
night

I don't want you to think
Geo. is perfect
Can throw little tantrums
hits the wall with his fist
about every 15 yrs.
likes to occasionally slam
doors

favorite curse words
golly ding
dad blast it
God bless a billie goat

(Jackie wrote this for my retirement)
- George

43

lope ask

Retirement worries? none
none except having enough
money to buy books

Family #1
nature activities
wild life - fawn   bats
         hawks   baby pigs
         snakes
                     dogs
                     horses
         plant farm cows
                     garden

Friends   always concerned
                     calls to check
swimming party
4th of July
New Year's Eve

Travel
    walking trips
Canoe
trips

Your Marriott Awaits℠
For reservations or information visit Marriott.com
or call 1 800 228 9290

I didn't know it then, but I believe now, that the Lord put Geo. in that place at that time or maybe none of us would be here today

Geo. went to the best in business Dr. William Orr + because Dr. Orr loved Geo. so much, he came to Col. and helped save and build that ar Clinic (Service).

George's finest qualities –
gathering good people around him
having faith in people
never losing sight of people's needs
– dreamer + planner
– mind never stops – can drive you crazy

The big shocker is that he can't balance to business Check book.

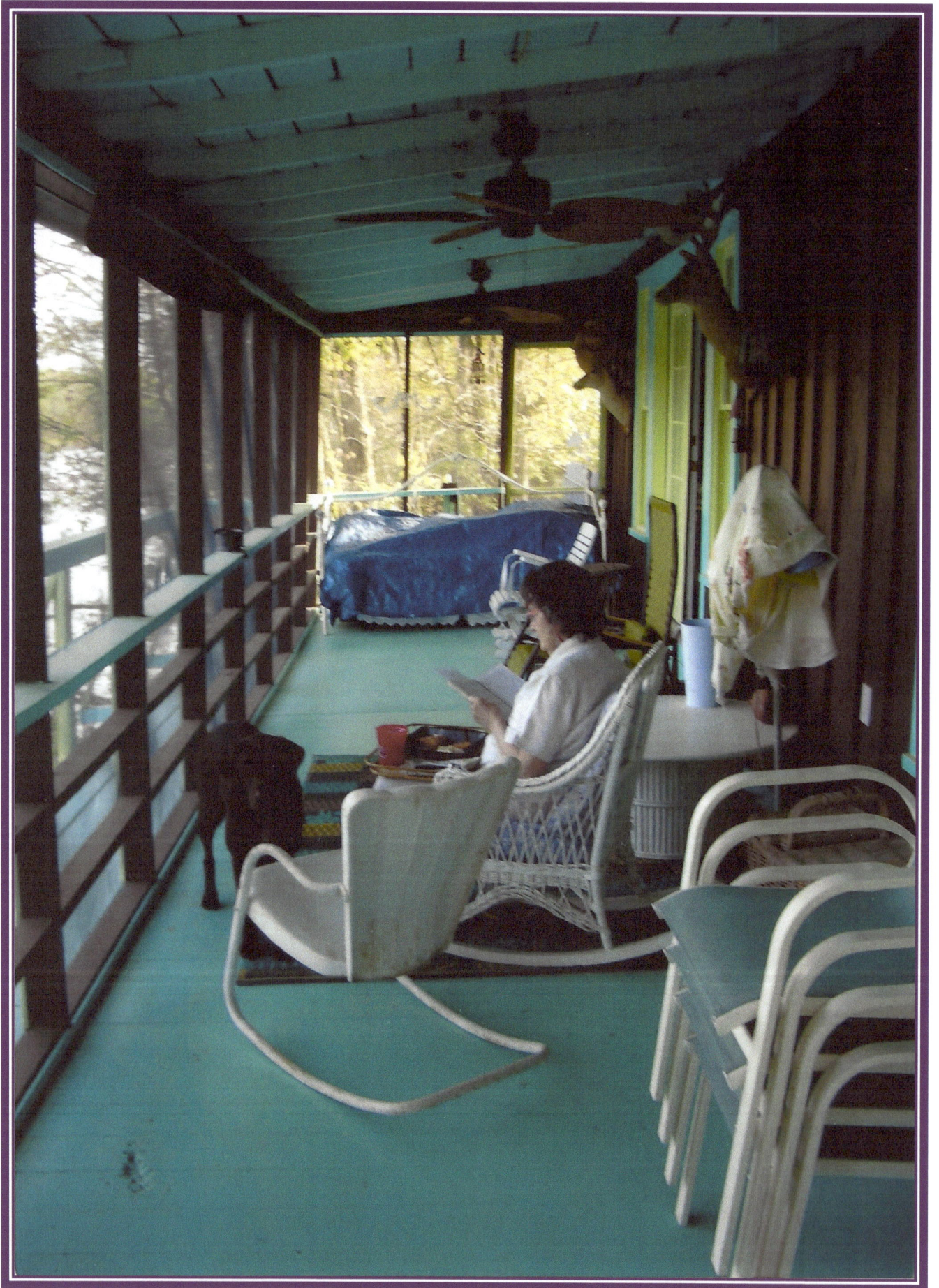

Jackie Spain

From:	"Trina Flynn" <flynnt@ensworth.com>
To:	"Jackie Spain" <jgspain@bellsouth.net>
Sent:	Wednesday, February 17, 2010 2:13 PM
Subject:	FW: top of the mountain

This made me laugh and cry.
Praise her

From: Jackie Spain [mailto:jgspain@bellsouth.net]
Sent: Wednesday, July 02, 2008 10:16 AM
To: Trina Flynn
Subject: top of the mountain

What a way to wake up, with a call from Machu Pichu. I can see it through your eyes, clearly in my head, feel the sun and wind and touch the giant stones perfectly fit together. Of course the difference would be that I would be "clutching" the walls for fear of falling all the way to the bottom of the mountain!!!

What a great climax to the trip of a life time. You'll have to sign up now for next year's trip, no matter what it is!

We have heard very little from the Flynns, so they must be getting along pretty well. I send them some food. We see them at church. I think the Spain children enjoy it. Izzy sat in church with us last Sun We are looking forward to the 4th, but will miss Pearson. Lynch and Jesse are coming tomorrow night (I'll bet they will want to stay to see you arrive, if it's not too late!) I think Lillei and Leah are coming. They have walked Sally some Lillie has been busy with dance camp. She said she really enjoyed it.

I'ls hard to imagine that they are already talking about going back to school. Adam and Angie want to spend some time at Estill, to sort of wind down. Christy and faily will be there this week end, then Adam, during the week, and then Darwin the next week end, with some friends, with a boat, I think.they also have a tent for the kids.

I don't know when you will get these ems, but we are waiting anxiously for your return. I'm so excited that there will be no jet lag, unless your brain ends up in your butt!!!

Take care and stay safe and God BLESS YOU ALL! i WILL PRAY for your saftey til you arrive in your own home,

To my precious, beloved daughter.

LOVE, MAMA

Dear John(ny),

I'm sure that a distinguished gentleman, such as yourself, would prefer not to be called "Johnny", but it is certainly more natural for me. *One of Jackie's high school boy friends.*

I appreciate, so much, your encouraging letters and your self portrait. I am not surprised that you are a writer and not too surprised that you are a fine artist, but "mule skinner"? That really caught me off guard. It seems that you have taken on the total Texas persona. Jane showed me a picture, that I guess was in a paper, of you looking like a "sho nuff" cowboy." I suppose it is difficult to live in TX without some of the wild west rubbing off on you.

In 1999, George and I took a trip to Big Bend. I had been reading about it and planned our trip. On the way down, we just rambled around on the old highways. We passed Austin by and stopped in San Antonio. It happened to be Cinco de Mayo, so it was very colorful and exciting. We did all the regular tourist things, but now I'm sorry we couldn't stay longer and see some gardens and surrounding country. We had an appointment with the Rio Grande.

We stayed in Terlingua in the old west hotel. We signed up for a river trip. The brochure showed the river rafts careening down the rapids, but we had to "paddle our own canoe". It was already May and hot! The guide said to get that kind of water and miss the heat, we should have been there in Feb. Or March. George kept saying, "we have to paddle ourselves, can you do it?" That's what we came to do and I wasn't about to let something like age stand in the way.

We took the trip through the Elena Canyon. It was so beautiful. We stopped on the Mexico side for lunch and took a hike up through some rocks. It was literally through a big hole in the rock, that water was coming through. We ended up on a huge smooth boulder where we could lie down in the shade and watch an eagle soaring–it turned out to be some special kind of buzzard!

The trip took most of the day going up river and then back down. I must say the old couple were the only ones that didn't go into the drink. It would have been embarrassing since the water in the rapids was only about knee deep. The spot where we put in, looked just like a scene in "Streets of Laredo", where they cross the Rio Grande.

We saw an interesting thing in Terlingua. There was a tiny church with a sign that had the Catholic Church and meeting time, then the Episcopal Church and time, and then the Church of Christ and meeting time. We thought the church on the border of Texas was much more progressive than some in middle TN. I wish it had been Sunday. It would have been interesting to see what kind of folks these were.

When we left Big Bend we too drove on to Marathon and stayed at the Gage Hotel. What a surprise, seemingly in the middle of nowhere. So beautiful!

It is spectacular country. I was stopping often to take pictures of rocks and flora. After we left the park, I looked for a rock to take home. I finally saw one that looked manageable on the side of the road. They are unusually heavy. Poor G nearly broke his back getting it into the trunk.

We also raised Great Danes, when we lived in the country. We've had many dogs since then, but now I have a chocolate Lab. She is so sweet and I feel very lucky that her disposition is so calm, since reading "Marley And Me". It seems that they can be crazy. She is energetic and does some of the same puppylike things, but not so destructive. Of course, she loves going to Estill and swimming in the lake.

I have my 3rd cycle of chemo this Mon. I have 3 consecutive days, 4 hrs. each day, every 28 days. The side effects were not nearly as bad the second time, so I'm each time will be a little easier. I'll be half way through, if all goes as we hope. I feel very well, just not as energetic as usual, but we are trying to walk at the Green Hills Mall when it is so cold.

I'm so thankful that your health has improved so. I know it has been a long, hard road. Having the love and support of your family is what means so much during those times. We often wonder how in the world people that don't have anyone get along.

God bless you and yours, Jackie

Jackie
Feb. 6, 2007

Jackie's Words for College Reunion

WHAT HAVE YOU BEEN DOING FOR THE LAST 50 YEARS?
Please complete and mail (EVEN IF NOT ABLE TO ATTEND) to:
LU Alumni Office; One University Park Drive; Nashville, TN 37204.
Information will be compiled into a booklet.

PERSONAL INFORMATION:

Name: First _Jacqulyn_ Middle/ Maiden _Burton_ Last _Spain_

Mailing Address _1724 N. Observatory Dr_

City _Nashville_ State _TN_ Zip _37215_

E-Mail Address _jcspain@bellsouth.net_ Phone _615-292-2845_

Spouse Name _George E. Spain_ Date of Marriage _June 22, 1958_

Children # _6_ Grandchildren # _13_ Great Grandchildren # _____

Additional education _____

Occupation _____

Position _____ Retired _____

Hobbies _Gardening_

LIPSCOMB MEMORIES:

Why did you come to Lipscomb? _Always planned to come to Lipscomb since a little girl._

Favorite Teacher _Jenny Ditty Brown / Sara Whitten_ Favorite Class _labs + sewing_

Favorite memories of Lipscomb _When I first met George - the first day I arrived to move into the dorm, he was sitting on the steps, checking out all the freshman girls._

Funniest thing that happened to you at Lipscomb _____

Most embarrassing moment at Lipscomb _____

Briefly share some of your experiences from the last 50 years _raising our family, playing farm for 20 years Now enjoying grandchildren, some travel. Retirement Now health issues (cancer)_

50

(615) 388-6653

**COLUMBIA AREA MENTAL HEALTH CENTER
OF CENTRAL TENNESSEE**

TROTWOOD AVENUE
P. O. BOX 1197
COLUMBIA, TENNESSEE 38401

Nov. 1, 1982

Dearest Jackie — my love

Sometimes — like this morning, when I'm by myself, something causes me to think of you so much and so hard I almost hurt inside loving you, especially as I think of our growing older together. It seems we have been together forever — and I cannot imagine you not being with me all these years — I love you more and more my dear dear wife — I love you, I love you

George

FOR THE EMOTIONAL AND SOCIAL PROBLEMS OF EVERYDAY LIVING

Dear George,

Centerstone
Community Mental Health Centers, Inc.

I thank God that you
are okay. I'm sure we
were both thinking the
same things, projecting
into the future, having
good times taken away
now. I guess we are
to the point where every
minute counts and I'm
so thankful that you don't
have to go through a bad
time now.

I'm thankful that you

are with me and I want
it to be a long time.
   I love you so much,
much more than I often
show.

          Jackie

          Aug 27, 2003

53

Recipe _Chocolate Cake_
Source _Johnnie Coggee - 1963 about_
Preparation Time _____ Cooking Time _____ Serves _____

Ingredients _____ (real)

1 cup melted butter	2 cups butter milk
2 cups sugar	2 tsp. soda
2 eggs well beaten	3 cups flour
6-8 Tbsp. cocoa	1 tsp. vanilla

Directions _Mix butter, sugar, cocoa. add eggs one at a time + beat well. Mix soda + milk (will foam) - add alternately with flour. Mix well. add vanilla. Bake 350° for 45 min. 2 layers (put cake in freezer to cool fast - makes it more moist, too) (put in buttered, floured pans_

Frosting

1 2/3	C. sugar
1/4	tsp. cream of tartar
1/4	tsp. salt
1/2	C. hot water

Boil to hard ball stage (6-7 min. microwave). Beat 4 egg whites til stiff. add sugar mixture in a slow stream til peaks add vanilla — ice cake

My favorite ways to serve this are with: _____
or over: _____
What did everyone like/dislike about it? _____

A good variation might be: _____
Can this be frozen and easily reheated? _____
Can I increase this easily to serve more people? _____
Additional comments: _____

Our traditional Birthday Cake all these years since Johnnie worked for us + made it for us.

The Best Damn Beans
(According to Buford Spain)

1   7 lb. can pork n beans
1   box dark brown sugar
1/2   cup Worchestershire sauce
2 or 3 heaping tablespoon mustard
1   large onion - chopped
1/2   lb bacon cut up
1/2   teas. ground cloves (or to taste)

Stir real well and bake uncovered 350° - 400° (depending on how much time you have) About 2-3 hrs. til thickened. Turn up heat if needed - they will thicken more as they cool off, so if you

over cook + they seem dry you can add water.

If I double recipe allow more baking time. (maybe 4 hrs.) this makes a large roasting pan.

Spray pan with Pam - helps clean up! Stir occasionally during baking.

Jackie Spain

55

Words About Her

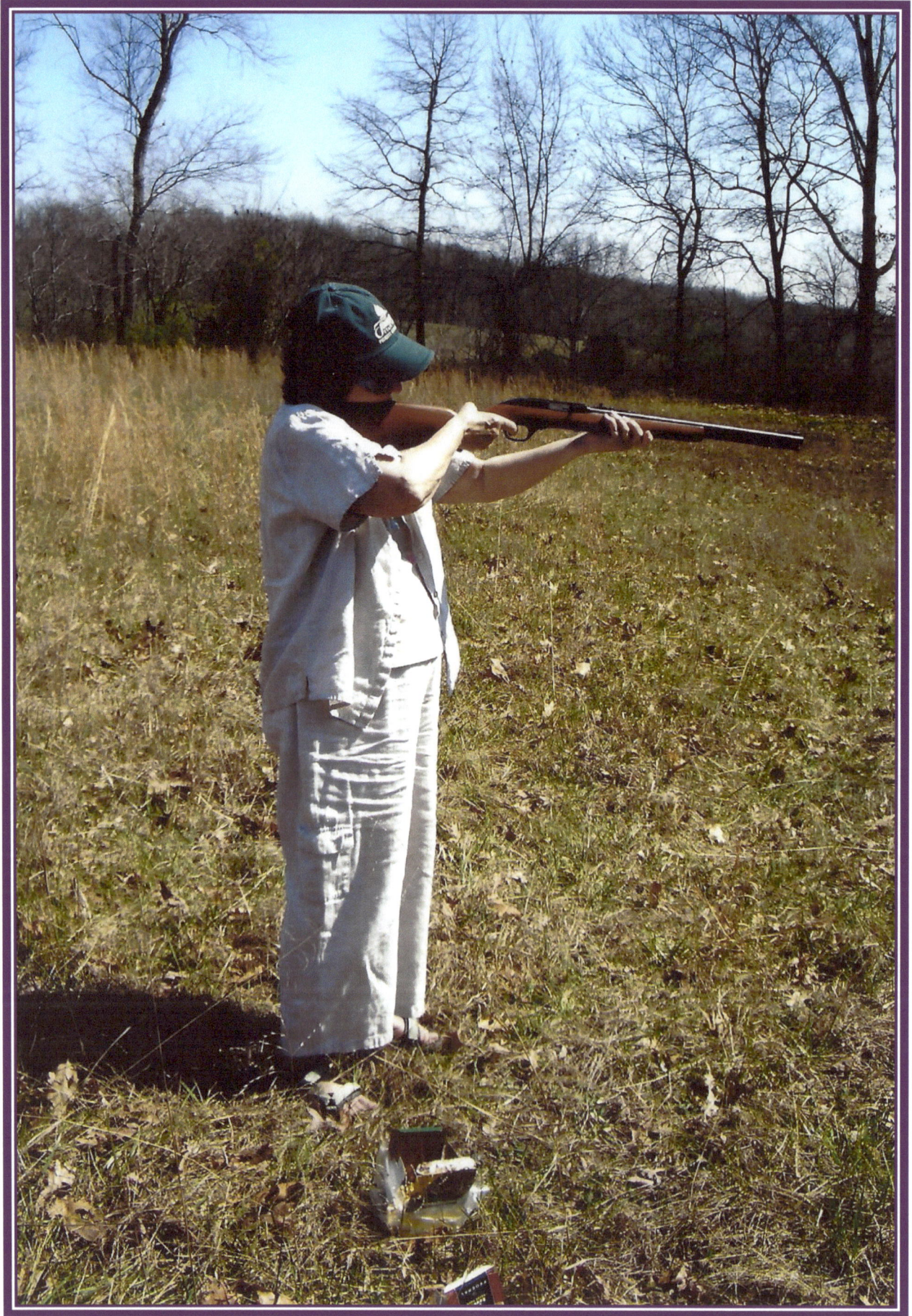

WINCHESTER OLIN MATHIESON CHEMICAL CORPORATION *Western*
TRADE-MARK

EAST ALTON, ILLINOIS

July 31, 1958

Mrs. Jackie B. Spain
1102 Maplehurst
Nashville, Tennessee

Dear Mrs. Spain:

H. D. Avery, our representative, has in-
formed us of your win at the recent Tennessee State
Skeet Shoot. Nice shooting! Needless to say, we
appreciate your confidence in WESTERN shells and a
WINCHESTER gun in your enjoyment of the shooting game.

Please accept our congratulations, and as
a token of our appreciation for the part which our
products were allowed to play, we are enclosing a
1958 WINCHESTER Blue Ribbon and a 1958 WESTERN
Champions Club for your shooting jacket. It is
hoped that we will find your name high on the
list of winners in the tournaments to come.

Wishing you continued success in the
shooting game, we remain

Yours very truly,

OLIN MATHIESON CHEMICAL CORPORATION
WINCHESTER-WESTERN Division

Cliff Doughman

Manager, Trap and Skeet
Shooting Promotion Department

C. B. Doughman/rls

Nashville's 'Dead Eye Dora' Is Ready for Dove Season

By BOB STEBER
TENNESSEAN Outdoor Editor

PETITE, pretty and a "Dead Eye Dora" with a shotgun is Jacqulyn (Mrs. George) Spain.

Black mineral dust puffed against the blue sky backdrop of the skeet range—just another flying target atomized by the young Nashville matron's accuracy with the scattergun.

Unperturbed by the cameraman's popping flashbulbs, Jackie was shooting and scoring high one recent Saturday at the Nashville Gun club's range at Berry field.

The brunette beauty's aplomb was amazing. She almost ran a perfect 25 despite the distraction of knowing the Cyclops eye of the camera was winking its mechanical eye at her every shot.

Jackie, along with her family, has been getting ready for opening of the dove season next Monday.

She's the daughter of Mr. and Mrs. Nelson Burton of Estill Springs, Tenn., has been shotgunning since she was barrelhigh to a .410.

It was at the age of 12 that Jackie started pulverizing clay pigeons at the Memphis skeet club. She won the City Junior crown at the age of 13 and the State Junior crown when 14.

It was just about that time that the family moved to a farm at Estill Springs, near Winchester, and she stopped formal shooting for the field variety.

Her mother is a former state ladies' skeet champion. Her brother, A. M. Burton II, was on the All America Junior team in 1948.

Jackie's brother, Nelson Jr., was too busy playing football for Vanderbilt to take much interest in range shooting, but he's a good field shot.

Nelson Sr.? "I'm just the coach," he laughs. "Memphis City runnerup was about the best I could ever do."

Jackie has two shooting goals —to win the state and run a perfect score at skeet.

She was runnerup for the State championship this year, shooting 84x100 on rounds of 19-21-21-23, missing the crown by just two birds.

Her best round is a 24 scored at the Nashville range just after the State. Jackie posted a fine 47x50 score that day.

She is a student at Nashville's David Lipscomb college. That's where she met her husband, George Edward Spain.

"Some of our earliest dates were on dove hunts," Jackie said.

"Lovey-dovey hunts, you mean," her dad chimed in and Jackie laughed merrily.

Jackie likes dove hunting best. "My feet get too cold on duck hunts," she confided. "But George has promised to get me some electric socks for this winter. We hope to hunt in Arkansas during the Christmas holi-

She is a student at Nashville's David Lipscomb college. That's where she met her husband, George Edward Spain.

"Some of our earliest dates were on dove hunts," Jackie said.

"Lovey-dovey hunts, you mean," her dad chimed in and Jackie laughed merrily.

Jackie likes dove hunting best.

"My feet get too cold on duck hunts," she confided. "But George has promised to get me some electric socks for this winter. We hope to hunt in Arkansas during the Christmas holidays."

Rabbit or quail?

"I have hunted them, but it takes a lot more walking than I like to do, tires me too much," she said.

Jackie's advice to the increasing number of women taking up shotgunning is to get a "good, man-sized gun."

"They won't kick you badly if you hold them right, use a cushioned stock," she advised.

"I didn't really start shooting until I graduated to a 12-gauge gun," the 110-pound beauty smiled.

"Just don't be afraid of it, lean into the gun and hold it firmly against your shoulder," she said.

Jackie laughed. "First time I ever tried to shoot the big gun, I was just a little afraid of it. I leaned backward and when I pulled the trigger the gun's recoil banged my head against the high house.

"I never did THAT again," she smiled.

"How do I hit them?" Jackie restated the question.

"I don't think any shotgunner ever really knows what he does. I think I just keep my eye on the target or game, and keep swinging my gun until after I've pulled the trigger.

"Never, NEVER stop the gun, I do know that," she emphasized.

Not only is young Mrs. Spain an accomplished nimrod, but a flyrod fan as well.

Her best bass was 4½-pounder, tricked by a popping bug at the famed Tunica cutoff in Mississippi.

"If you want to shoot well, join a gun club," is Jackie's closing advice.

"I've noticed the club members like to help new shooters correct their faults. To be able to shoot well is the best part of hunting," she concluded.

Mrs. George Spain—Looking For A Perfect Score

Chattanoogans

(Continued From Preceding Page)

Roy Moore Jr. (149), Mack Brothers Jr. (150), Pier Morgan (151) and Bob Lowry Jr. (151).

John Deal, the Old Hickory star who was figured as Nashville's top threat, withdrew after the first nine in the afternoon. John had a 78 in the morning and was several over par when he decided to pick up.

The qualifying scores:

146—Bill Davidson (Belle Meade) 70-76; Ed Brantley (Chattanooga) 74-72.

148—Wesley Brown (Chattanooga) 79-69.

149—Marshall Trammell (Belle Meade) 77-72; Roy Moore Jr. (Memphis) 73-76.

150—Mack Brothers Jr. (Belle Meade) 75-75.

151—Pier Morgan (Chattanooga) 73-78; Robert Lowry Jr. (Huntsville) 75-76.

155—Les Cater (Knoxville) 75-80.

156—Richard Spencer (Huntsville) 80-76.

158—Hugh Goodman Jr. (Chattanooga) 78-80.

161—Robert Lowry Sr. (Huntsville) 79-82.

164—Brock Stokes (Richland) 82-82;

Bill Scheffer (Richland) 79-ell (Chattanooga) 81-83.

166—Bill Condon (Memphis)

169—Joe Orrill III (Memphis)

171—Charles Kittle (Memphis)

173—Jere Whitson (Cookeville)

Withdrew—John Deal (Old

Did Not Start—Hall Thompson Meade), Herreld Kirkpatrick Ky.), DeWitt Thompson III Meade).

U. S. Bids To Host '65 Silent Olympics

MILAN — (AP) — The manager the American squad at the Silent Olympics said yesterday United States would bid to h the games in 1965 in Washington D. C.

The Silent Olympics—the in national games for the deaf— held every four years. The n and ninth edition of the gar

Culinary Artistry C

By SARAH HOLLY
Food Editor

Killing rattlesnakes is routine for Mrs. George E. Spain.

But keeping a watch for these unwelcome guests who occasionally slither through the back yard is the only drawback, Mrs. Spain said, of living in a secluded country location.

The Spains live on Waddell Road, which is off—way off—Old Hillsboro Road. You find your way there over a maze of twisting gravel roads, the last of which turns out to be an extremely long driveway that winds up a hill and back into the woods.

Then suddenly, there it is—an English-style country manor. You are met by a Great Dane or two and an assortment of Beagles. Crossing the courtyard you are welcomed by two beautiful little boys and a tiny, talkative girl.

Stepping into the house is like taking a giant step backwards in time, into a gentler era of gracious living in an atmosphere of relaxed formality.

"We always wanted to live in the country," Mrs. Spain said. "We knew the type of setting we wanted — lots of pretty hills and woods. We patterned our house after the English country style and got our ideas by looking at hundreds of pictures."

Mrs. Spain, the former Jacquiyn Burton, daughter of Mr. and Mrs. Nelson Burton, was born in Nashville and majored in home economics at David Lipscomb College.

In 1956 she was married to George Edward Spain, son of Mr. and Mrs. George J. Spain. George, a graduate of David Lipscomb College and the University of Tennessee School of Social Work, is now a psychiatric social worker at Vanderbilt Hospital.

Their three children, Brad, 5, Lynch, 4, and Trina, 2, love their country home where hummingbirds hover right outside the den windows and brilliant Indigo Buntings dip through the forrest trees which surround the house.

George relaxes by riding horseback over the hills and in season he grabs his favorite shotgun and goes hunting.

The Spains have a large vegetable garden and raise their own chickens. Winter finds the freezer packed with fresh vegetables, fryers and a side of beef.

Entertaining at the Spain's is usually informal, although the dining room, which is papered in red, features a banquet-sized table.

"We like buffets," Mrs. Spain said. "Our favorite form of entertaining is to have our friends over for dinner. We always get into big discussions and that provides the entertainment. Conversation isn't a lost art with us."

Here are a few of Mrs. Spain's favorite recipes:

Spicy Ham Steak

Center slices of ham, an inch thick, are used in this dish, which is best cooked on the charcoal grill. You'll need:
¼ cup melted butter
1 cup sherry
1 cup pineapple juice
2 teaspoons ground cloves
¼ cup dry mustard
¼ cup packed brown sugar
2 teaspoons paprika
1½ cloves garlic, minced
Combine all ingredients, slash edges of ham, and marinate three hours, turning several times. Grill 20 minutes, basting occasionally.

Frozen Fruit Salad

Delicious party fare, this creamy rich salad serves 20. You'll need:
1 cup apricots
1 cup peaches
1 cup pineapple chunks
1 cup Queen Ann cherries
½ pound marshmallows
2 cups cream, whipped
1 cup almonds or pecans
3 oranges
2 cups mayonnaise
Drain fruit and cut into chunks. Combine whipped cream and mayonnaise. Add fruit and nuts. Freeze until very firm.

Lemon Mint Butter

Great with green peas, this is also good on small cooked onions or a combination of peas and tiny whole carrots. You'll need:
½ cup soft butter
1 tablespoon lemon juice
¼ teaspoon grated lemon peel
2 to 3 tablespoons finely chopped fresh mint
Cream the butter with lemon juice and peel. Add mint. Melt the flavored butter generously over hot cooked peas just before serving.

Refrigerator Rolls

The beauty of this recipe is that the dough can be kept in the refrigerator, allowing these rolls to be made well in advance. They must, however, be allowed to rise two hours before cooking. You'll need:
¾ cup sugar
¾ cup melted shortening
1½ cups warm sweet milk
1 yeast cake, dissolved in ½ cup warm water
2 eggs, beaten
Mix all ingredients. Add flour to make waffle-like batter. Let rise 2 hours. Then add 1 teaspoon salt and flour to make like sticky biscuit dough. Refrigerate until thoroughly chilled. Cut out rolls and allow to rise 2 hours before cooking. Butter generously with melted butter. Bake at 400 degrees until golden brown.

Wine Jello

A sophisticated version of an old favorite. You'll need:
1 small package strawberry Jello
1½ cups boiling water
½ cup any sweet red wine
Dissolve Jello in boiling water; add the wine. Chill until set. Serve topped with whipped cream. Serves 4.

Baked Bean Casserole

Cool weather—believe it or not—is only a few weeks away. And what tastes better on a crispy day than hot baked beans? You'll need:
8 bacon slices
4 large onions
½ to 1 cup brown sugar
1 teaspoon dry mustard
½ teaspoon garlic powder
1 teaspoon salt
½ cup cider vinegar
2 cans (15 ounce) dried lima beans, drained
1 pound can green lima beans, drained
1 pound can red kidney beans, drained
1 pound-11-ounce can New England style baked beans
Fry bacon until crisp. Remove from skillet and brown onion. Add sugar and other ingredients except beans. Cook this mixture 20 minutes uncovered. Add to beans. Add crumbled bacon. Bake in a 3-quart casserole at 350 degrees for 1 hour. Serves 12.

Soliere, Bohannon Vows Told

Grace Nazarene Church was the scene July 31 of the wedding of Miss Carolyn Bohannon, daughter of Mrs. Verna Bohannon and Ray Bohannon of Romulus, Mich., to Gary Soliere, son of Mr. and Mrs. John R. Soliere of Phoenix, Ariz. George Scott, pastor of the church, officiated.

The bride, given in mar-

riag
Hay
Mi
the
Char
A

Comes from Country Kitchen

—Staff colorphoto by Jimmy Holt

A beautiful meal in a beautiful setting is part of the formula for gracious living in the country home of Mr. and Mrs. George E. Spain. Here a guest-tempting buffet of Spicy Ham Steak, Frozen Fruit Salad, Peas with Lemon Mint Butter, hot rolls and Wine Jello has been prepared by Mrs. Spain.

riage by her uncle, Arthur Hayes, wore full bridal attire.

Miss Peggy Dixon served as the bride's only attendant. Charles Cassady was best man. A reception was given by

the bride's aunt, Mrs. Arthur Hayes, immediately after the ceremony.

After a wedding trip, Mr. Soliere and his bride will make their home in Phoenix.

63

Thursday, July 31, 1975

Jackie Spain—A Lady in the Woods

by Jody Buckley

Jackie Spain is refreshing . . . mainly because she is just like everyone else. "I'm certainly not the Super Woman that some of the other people you've written about are," she said laughing, "I'm just an ordinary mother of five who does the laundry and the meals." Being the mother of five can be spectacular in its own right . . . but it is even more so when you have to keep track of three dogs, chickens, horses, a pet hawk and a husband. The Spains and their animal friends inhabit some lovely wooded acres on Stillhouse Hollow Road which is the same as Fire Tower Road which is in an area of Williamson County known as Rattlesnake Hollow. Getting there is half the battle.

Born in Memphis, Jackie Burton, and her parents moved to Franklin County when she was a young girl. She attended high school there and was graduated from David Lipscomb College in Nashville where she majored in Home Economics and met George Spain. After their marriage, in 1956, they lived for several years in Nashville and then began to, as she says, ". . . roam Williamson County for a place to build. I was just pregnant at the time and didn't care much for riding around country roads, so George and Billy Billington rode around for weeks until they found this land."

And the forested woodlands surrounding their home provide the setting that shows off their home. The drive approaching their house is a paved forest path that twists and turns beneath the trees. One is reminded of the line from Evangeline by Longfellow "This is the forest primeval; the murmuring pines and the hemlocks; Bearded with moss and in garments green-indistinct in the twilight."

A Tree House

At the end of this poetic drive is a large house of gray barn siding and red painted window sills and doors and it sits appropriately there not intruding on nature . . . not interrupting its flow.

The house itself was built 13 years ago and sprang from George Spain's doodling pad. "George is quite artistic,and for years we had been collecting pictures and sketches about homes," Jackie recalled, "and during some long meeting, George began to doodle and this is what he drew!" Sure enough on a little 3" by 5" scratch piece of paper is their house . . . perfectly matched in detail by the house that now stands.

"When we first began building the house here, just about everyone thought we were crazy. Much of the land was rough and scrubby and of course, the people who live around here all told us about the rattlesnakes here," she said.

Rattlesnakes to the contrary (although there are two large tanned rattlesnake skins that are in evidence in the house and one large rattlesnake in the freezer (frozen stiff), the Spains persisted and finally moved in with their two boys and a baby Trina who was 6 months old.

The move was accomplished right before Christmas, 1962, and there are many people still living who remember that Christmas. Fourteen inches of snow blanketed the county and kept everybody from running to the store. But, apparently, it was a warm, quiet Christmas Eve for the Spains in their new house in the country. "It is truly the nicest Christmas I can recall. Our friends in Nashville would call us to make the usual Christmas party circuit," she recalls gleefully, "and I had to tell them I was SNOWED IN! . . we were stranded here and loved it."

Comfortable Plus

The house would be a nice one to be stranded in. The living room is filled with shelves of comfortable-looking books on one wall that faces a wall of huge rough-cut stone around a large floor to ceiling window. The woods outside come right up to the house as though asking to be let in. Also throughout the house are handsome wildlife prints and Indian art, three bobcat skins, some good deep chairs and a lot of exposed beams in the ceilings.

Each room has some particularly outstanding feature that sets it apart from the rest. A small parlor-type room off the entrance hall has an old whale-oil chandelier; the dining room has a magnificent long oak dining table and rough sawn fir paneling. The den is now what used to be the breezeway and has a stone floor and a riot of plants and fern. Upstairs, the master bedroom has a vaulted cathedral ceiling and a huge picture window that overlooks a forest.

There is a lot of life built into that house and a lot of living goes on there. The aforementioned children are: Brad 16½, Lynch, 15, Trina, 13, Adam 9, and Darwin, 6. Every night seven people sit down to dinner. There is laundry and sewing and cleaning to be done for seven people . . . and once they raised two baby pigs in the entrance hall.

Jackie Spain has adapted herself to the clamorings of children, dogs as well as to the creepiness of snakes and assorted woods creature. She also fits easily into the role of actively concerned citizen. She is on the boards of the Williamson County Counseling Center and the Day Care Center. She sincerely believes that these centers give deprived children a glimpse into a better life.

Her interest in social problems has been stimulated by her husband's occupation as psychiatric social worker at a clinic in Columbia. She is proud of his work at the clinic and his success in the counseling field and is supportive of his efforts to help families discuss their problems and seek solutions. "You can't tell me that families don't have problems. I KNOW that they do but it helps to talk them out or to seek some advice. More people should realize that."

Jackie Spain's problems are of the usual kind—things like sons bringing home dead bobcats and rattlesnakes and the problem of having to tear down part of the house to move in a huge grandfather's cupboard.

But she has a way of observing life as it happens around her and of learning from it. Squirrels and rabbits are just as much a part of her day as children and chores . . . and she looks at life in general with a calmness and a wit that is refreshing.

This is the front of the Spain's attractive home on Stillhouse Hollow Road. The plans for the home sprang from George Spain's doodling pad and today is an unusual blending of gray siding wood and bright red painted doorways and window frames. Wildlife, plants and trees abound.

All photos by Jody Buckley

One wall of the comfortable den and living room features Indian prints, dried arrangements and three bobcat skins. The cats were found in the area of the Spain's home.

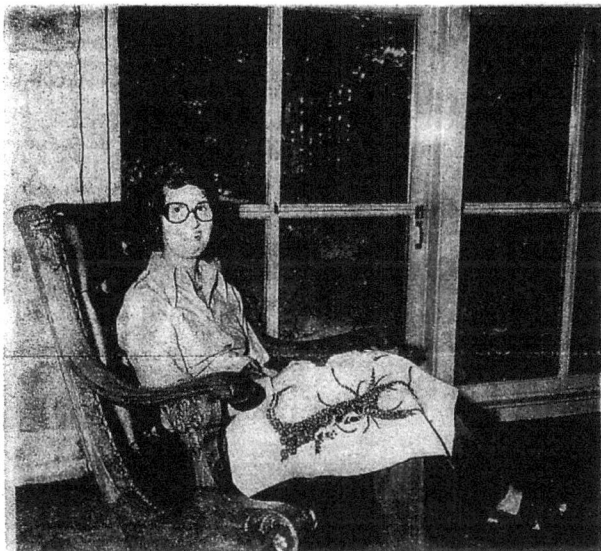
Jackie is shown here with her two youngest sons Adam, age 9 and Darwin, age 6, on their back lawn accompanied by the family dog. Beside them is the fence that surrounds a large pool which is a lifesaver when a passle of kids meet up with a hot summer day.

Jackie Spain is shown here in front of the large picture window that is the focal point of the large attractive den in her home. Her hobbies are needlepoint and 5 children and reading when she can.

65

Jackie's Poem

Hawkwild blue day,
Wings spread the breeze,
Soar, stoop away.

White chickens run
Under tall trees
Cackling their fun.

Golden butter,
Her strong hands squeeze
Out the water.

Red swing fly high,
The shark deep seas
Below us lie.

A rattlesnake
She smites with ease,
Then bakes a cake.

Listen! The drone
Songs of fairies
Under moss-stone.

Wife and mother,
For both of these
Tears and laughter.

Beautiful dove,
You I would please,
My life, my love.

Lying Here

Lying here
On our living room floor

Warm and well
Smoking my Oom Paul

Getting a little heady

This Thanksgiving 1969
Im trying to write
A poem worth reading
100 yrs from now
Or at least next week

Something moving
Pulls my attention
Outside to the woods
And through 12
Large window panes
I begin watching
Last summers leaves

Floating   falling
Brown and dry

They pile on top
Of others lying there
And begin to disappear

It makes me a little sad
Knowing

But for the moment
Im warm and well
And hear our children
Fussing and laughing

And your footsteps
In the bedroom above me

- Jackie

I want you to be here in the morning,
Warm and well and asleep,
In the bed beside me.

I want you to be here,
Just around the corner in the hall,
In your orange robe and gray slippers.

I want you to be here, so near
I can hear your beautiful voice say,
"Bubba's is my coffee ready?"

I want you to be here on the couch,
With Sally's head resting on your lap,
And see your hand reach out and pat her.

I want you to be here with me now,
Wiping the tears from my eyes,
So I can see you clearly.

I want you to be here beside me now,
Where I can feel you and hear you,
Saying, over and over, again and again,
"Bubbas, my dear Bubbas, you're so precious.

                    to Jackie my Babes" - George 9-15-09

OUR MAMA –

OUR MAMA COULD –

- TOUCH THE TIP OF HER NOSE WITH HER TONGUE.
- FIND HER WAY ALL OVER MEMPHIS, TN. THROUGH THE STORM SEWER SYSTEM AS A CHILD.
- WADE THROUGH ICY SWAMPS IN ARKANSAS IN WINTER FOLLOWING HER FATHER AND BROTHERS ON DUCK HUNTS.
- PEE OVER THE SIDE OF A BOAT IN MISSISSIPPI BACKWATERS EVEN UNDER THE THREAT OF BEING GRABBED BY GIANT ALLIGATOR GAR FISH.
- RIDE A HORSE WITH A BROKEN ARM
- SWITCH DRIVERS IN A '57 T-BIRD BY CLIMBING OUT THE DRIVERS WINDOW AND GOING OVER THE TOP AND BACK INTO THE PASSENGERS SIDE WINDOW WHILE SPEEDING DOWN THE BEACH IN FLA.
- BEAT EVERY OTHER GIRL IN FRANKLIN CO. IN FOOT RACE CONTESTS
- OUT SHOOT <u>ALL</u> THE WOMEN AND MOST OF THE MEN IN THE STATE OF TN. 4 YRS. IN A ROW (SKEET - SHOTGUN).
- RAISE FIVE WILD KIDS THE RIGHT WAY.
- RAISE A GARDEN - VEGITABLE AND FLOWER GARDENS.
- MILK A COW
- CAN VEGITABLES
- MAKE CHEESE, BUTTER, COTTAGE CHEESE, ETC.
- RAISE FUNNY CHICKENS
- TOLERATE ALL MANNER OF ANIMALS IN THE HOUSE - ALIVE AND DEAD
- TOLERATE ALL MANNER OF PEOPLE IN THE HOUSE
- NEVER TELL A LIE
- BE VERY FUNNY   ACCEPTING
- BE VERY SERIOUS
- "   "   WISE
- "   "   DEPENDABLE
- "   "   LOYAL
- "   "   FEARLESS
- NEVER FALTER IN FAITH   *SEE FEARLESS
- FIGHT SATAN - CALL HIM OUT TO DO BATTLE OVER HER CHILDRENS LIVES

BEAT TWO OTHER MEN WHILE WATER-SKIING ON THE ELK RIVER

68

- Always positive in the face of adversity
- Always fair with people
- Voice her opinion — even if it was tough to hear
- Pick art. Had a great eye for art.
- Good music critic also
- Maintain healthy relationships w/ friends and family that lasted many decades.
- Evaluate difficult and terrifying situations and quickly make firm and sound decisions then proceed on without regret.
- Not look back only forward — see above
- Be gentle kind and sweet. To animals and people
- Compassionate, empathetic, sympathetic.
- A fierce competitor
- Someone you did not want to tangle with (usually she was right and you were wrong)
- An unyielding force if the situation called for it.
- Very flexible and yielding if the situation called for it.
- Your fortress to retreat to if you needed to
- Your greatest defender
- The one example you could and should aspire to be more like in this lifetime.
- Understood the profound gift of life and conciousness and lived it to the fullest.

2009

Dear Daddy,   6-12-09

    I'm glad you've asked that these
memories be written down now. At some
time I feel certain we'd have begun
this, but better at this time. There
are so many.

    One that came to me last night
was at the table. Maybe we had
finished supper. I can't remember
what we had but I bet it was good.
Maybe fried chicken. That's a wild
guess and I say that cause it was
a favorite. Remember how Mama
would put all the fried pieces
that fell off the chicken into a
small bowl or tiny plate and let
us eat them. She let us snack
on them as she cooked. I loved
those so. It was just the chunks of
batter that fell of the chicken
and had fried crisp. Regardless

    Regardless. After we finished
supper Mama or you said you had
a big surprise about something
we were going to get. I don't guess
Adam would have said much as

smiling real big. Probably dog and horse came out quickly and Brad right off said a baby. I do remember how happy and excited y'all were. All of us, that Darwin was on his way.

Another was at the table. Really two. It seems that these started during supper and continued with us all there long afterward. It was two great arguments. The greatest being about the porpise (sp) and dolphin and the other I think on the blunderbuss. The first being the most famous. The second I'm not sure of but it strikes a memory.

I have that table. It was Grandma Pearson's table, Mama's grandmother. We at there and Mama would put our Easter Egg baskets there, big Valentines Day card, and birthday presents. We still do much of the same.

I think we sat

Trina Mama
x x
& Daddy

After the breezeway was closed off we sat there a good bit after supper. Remember how Raven and Elijah would come up so shy and lay their heads in Mama's lap. You sat in the big chair next to the couch and Mama on the couch as you did in Nashville. After a short bit here came one paw, then another then the tail end. It was all so funny we couldn't say no and would always laugh until they passed gas running us all off.

How many Mamas would allow so many fresh killed snakes, birds, and animals to be placed in their freezers. Rattlesnakes, various hawks and woodpeckers, rabbits, squirrel, fox, and bob cats. What did your friends think. I can imagine them being shown at parties with lots of jokes followed by maybe real light fussing from Mama even though she was really proud. Proud because ya'll had a life that no others had. We all did.

4

Did Mama know she was getting
Beauty? Probably not and how you
pulled that off is a story in itself.
Even though she was a Christmas
present for Mama it was so exciting
for us all. I imagine you got that
English saddle with the squede
at the knees but I'm not sure.
She was tied up to one of the dragon
head post next to the gardens
gate. The one on the left facing
the house, I think. Probably
ya'll went riding later. We all
rode that morning up and down the
driveway.

Growing up the garden was always
as I remember magical. The fountain,
gates and wall made the area another
world. I bet the grandchildren
thought the same about Nashville.
Mama let us keep the ground hog
there in its cage.

It seems we always had many
visitors at our house. For living
so far out I just remember lots
of people. I guess cause ya'll were

the people, folks wanted to be around.
There as in Nashville it seemed the
same. Begin in the kitchen then
to the library. The library just
happens to be in the living room now.
Even at gatherings away from home
people were always near ya'll. You
were not dull and people desired to
be your friends. It always was the
same with Trinie, very natural. Ya'll
didn't try to make it that way, it just
was.

We are a family that tells stories.
Those of our people are different. Lots
of folks have to rely on the past but
our life created stories. You know
in the country the animals, certainly
the dogs and horses, were family.
It goes without saying the house
was, but even the land. How
many cousins chose to have parties
at our house? I think it was
all a part of one thing. People felt
peace and comfort. The nurse said
she felt that about Nashville.

party when we caught the hawk? Maybe not. Cathy Grant had a big one there.

It was a party. People tell me that I have an extroodinary family. I know that we do but have never thought on the subject in that way. It all seemed so natural and was. To put effort into making the many moments occur would have worn the nerves to a frazzle.

I'll write much more. Today I'll pick up a notebook. Daddy the adventure is far from over. Mama's presence is so strong in us all. Trina especially. But its you that comfort us. In every story you are there. Ya'll always were there.

With Only Love & Respect,

Yours Son Lynch

6-12-09

Memories about Mama of course
helping in the kitchen as a
child canning, vegetables, licking out
the cake bowls, helping make scrambled
eggs for dinner (one of the eggs had a
dead chick in it) Mama scooped it
out and said we won't tell anyone
about it. I probably disagreed in
my head but that is as close as
I remember I was only little and
thought it funny, also. Being made
to wear an XL cup for football
practice I've heard Pearson has a
cup story. I eventually quit wearing
it. Horse back riding. Remembering
Mama telling Lynch & Trina to
be good to Darwin and I while
Daddy/Mama went out for the
evening. I think I got the worst
of it seeing as Darwin was
younger. Always being at all the
football games for Darwin and me.
That was a lot. Laying in the
back or sitting in front of that
giant big blue truck.

by Adam

I remember the change from a
hand whipping to a belt whipping;
I should never laughed when her hand
stopped hurting my tail end.
Hunter is 22 lbs

I remember parties, trips, going off
to the Marines. She and Daddy
visiting Germany while Angie, Shane,
and I lived there. I believe it to
been around X-mas cause the X-mas
markets were open. That was a fun
time having them come there. She
would say one or two German words
stressing the sounds of course and
laugh or smile. She and I drove out
to see L, S, A, and Jessie at Pine
Ridge; we drove straight there. Loads of
talk time. I drove all but about
2 hrs. In the middle of S.D. the
pheasants tried to kill us She
did a hard swerve woke me up
and I got to drive again. Then
we ended up at the Res. as they
call it at maybe 2:00 A.M.
pulling up into some wild looking
places both of us thinking we will

77

She loved humming birds, one just
sucked on some water here in
Estill. Back to S.D. we did a few
hiking trips one up to Camel Mt,
Turtle MT., some kind of name like
that, Lynch would know. Maybe it
was Broke Back Mt. Anyway, the
path was up and down, one area
was like a bowl we had to
come back down she ran down it!
I thought oh my! You had to be
there to see the site. Like Daddy
said to me at Joe's Funeral, we
used to all call Mama for times, places,
and directions, and call to ask
how to cook a certain piece of beef
or cooking tip, at least I did.
I would call ~~to things I would~~
~~call for day times~~ to tell
about things A. had seen or done
for the day or week. We both got
into the T.V. series Lost and Prison
Break we both disliked Tea Bag out
of Prison Break he was a bad one.
Her plants, cakes, clothes, house,
All those great X-mas envelopes!

Here is one I'd of called Mama about. A hummingbird was eating then hovered about a foot away from the feeder but facing Ang and I had a poo and went back to the feeder. How many people have seen a hummingbird poo? She would take care of us, hold us, discipline us, praise us, laugh and cry with us, teach us, talk to us about God & Christ, talk to about bad habits, talk about nothing important, tell stories, talk of cooking to politics. She was the best back scratcher. Sometimes I think I need to call Mama then I'll remember that I can't.

This was written by Adam 8/09

Memories from Adam

Jackie Spain

From:	<abspain@yahoo.com>
To:	<jgspain@bellsouth.net>
Sent:	Friday, June 19, 2009 9:34 PM
Subject:	ma

I remember being in the baby room swimming in the pool with a starofoam bubble being helped with the chickens planting in the vegetable garden picking the vegetables strawberries and yellow squash being the worst to pick I remember Mama taking me and picking me up and a few times wondering if she remembered to get me from football practice. the first several years getting me in her giant blue truck with horns on top and big exhaust pipes down the sides.I remember having been made to wear a cup for football that was way to BIG for me.I remember thinking how beautiful she was when You and Mama went out with your friendsI remember helping her cook and can and getting to lick the bowl after magical hands had been through the kitchen what a great cook she was we will miss her cooking mmmmm along with fannies puddings and trinies breakfast i guess that is a good spot to stop next time i will probably over lap my life she gave us i will probably remember something else and have to start over in time mamas beans this weekend

I. Introduction

II. Why wel tell stories (Mother Lynch+Friends)

+ Mother Lynch telling stories
- Grandpa Lynch's brother kill brother being kill KMt.
- Mother L mam running off soldiers
- Peeing on drunk husband frozen to ground
- Father L. milking cow in dress
        ↓ Daddy
    Grand Daddy (Fannie's father)
    Georgie
    Papa Spain-Indian
    Georgie + Fannie
    Black Help (Pulling skonks from under house)

Trina + Dandy
        ↓
Buggy Top (Lost Cove)
                Witch
            Saul Mose Musador
        ↓
    Trips To mexico 1. Mama + Daddy
                2. Brad + Lynch
                3. Brad Lynch + Trina

Moving to Country
    Daddy
        ↓
    Neighbors 1. Bennetts
            2. Perrys
            3. Elams (Daddy Pulling Pole from lake)
            4. Mr. Washington (rooster laid eggs)
        ↓
    Animal Stories

82

- Bambi
- Catching Ground Hog on way to Church
- Raising pigs in oven/riding pigs
- Dogs
- Horses
- Snakes
- Hawks
- Chickens

Buggy Top Cave
- Daddy rappeling
- Trips way back in there
- As children

Trips
Daddy & Mama's trips to Mexico
Brad & Lynch
 Brad Lynch & Trina
Pickett
Adam's travels!
Mama & Daddys trips

South Dakota
    Ask Sara
Turkey Hunts
BigFoot Ride
Herding Horses
Children Playing Hooky

Fighting
Plane Crash Sean
Georgie & Papa Sp

Grandaddy on Wal

Civil War

Bennetts

Adam

age 5-7 riding Cindy in Franklin parade

games we played — run away slave,
duels with black powder pistols,
horse manuer/walnut fights, dead mouse fights
one-eyed feral cow, vege gardens
run away ponies, planting pine trees ② left over
swimming, walking past the Bennett's

Chicken baptisms // pet deer "Bambi"

Squierrel hunting, sitting with Daddy freezing
waiting on a deer that didn't show-up,
helping build dog house

Football

military - Germany, med floats, England

traveling =

Shane, Angie, Janet, Hunter, & St

Trinie's breakfast

Fannies puddings

trip to South Dakota with

Lost Cove trips

Ocoee Trips

- tell about trip to Montana
- Jackie whipping a Darwin
  Belt (Big Hole) ofk Pearsin saddle
- host Cove (Buggy to P tipping
- Chain Wm Tyrrel
- Solan : Angel (tiger trap) the Hunt
- Bob cat
- One-eyed wild cow
- Mexico Hunt in '63

Woods on fire.
Estill Springs - children lost on island
Cemetary picnics / Bell Witch
Falconry
tell about Georgie & Fannie, James Vann & Lewis P. Crosslin

(Xmas Jam)
riding horses —

canoeing

crawdad hunting

- sledding

- frozen pond

· Trinie's wedding / coal mine

Pickett

· Fat chicken

· Give me back my golden arm

milking cow — baby bird

- Mama's truck

- Sewing —

· Cooking —

· decorating

- Darwin — lashing darwin — tying him up —

· playing in mud —

- hidden stash of jewelry

- family, furniture

· pigs in oven

- Mama socking Cindy (the pony)
  in the nose

- summers — at 7 hills

- Mary stories

- rattlesnake at
  Mary's

- Brad's snake going to
  World's Fair

why we are
doing this —

Introduce ourselves

4 Pan over pictures
  in bedroom

(Make photos of
 rooms to include)

(Teaching me to
 water ski
 Jackie's skiing
 + shooting +
 beauty queen)

85

Georgie stories
toughness –

Daddy –
- origins of herd
- wedding
- horrible honeymoon
- memories of Tom Crossley - sitting in his lap –

Bell Witch Cemetary   ↘ his wife fought w/ Robert E
                                                        Lee
      James Vann   battles

- Mama + Papa Spain - Whiskey Making –

- old retarded guy –
- Fire Tower - Jack Martin machete
- Lady of Ill Fame

- King
- Perrys
- Bennetts
   - dead man hanging out of window

- Montana - Darwin - wiping w/ belt
- Wales / Germany / Sundance / Amazon / Churchhill /
Hurricain Andrew   Hudson Bay -
                                                    Rio Grande
Estill - Island - lost children
Pickett
Lost Cove / Buggy Top - <u>Daddy upside down</u>

Mexico — us w/ Dandy
          Dandy - Mexico - paranoia
Wild Cow

Hawks
Deer

pigs in dining room / in oven
Daddy w/ chicken killing dog - beating -
rattlesnack on hillside
snake in hole w/ school children
snake in house
fire in the woods .

Bennett Dogs walking home -
leaches on us from lake
road crew Still House

87

June 10, 2008

Mr. George Spain
1724 N. Observatory
Nashville, TN   37215

Dear George,

Just a note of hello. Tonight, June 10, 2008, I will say a special prayer for Jackie!
Let us pray that our great God will hear and answer it in the affirmative. He is
able to do exceedingly great things. He is still able to heal and renew. Let us
believe. Tell Jackie to meditate on him. He is a spirit and to let her spirit
talk to him. Ask her to use the power of the tongue to speak things as she wants
them to be.

George, I am one lazy man. I have not started to write. I will try again. Your
last letter will be read daily or weekly to get me started.

How is "Jackie's Garden", I hope it is the spirit of life. Gardening can be therapu-
tic for us all. Bringing to life plants is awesome. The beauty of flowers and plants
along with smell is exciting.

Things are going well for me. God has me content in this state of being. We all
travel thru the storms of life; prison, sickness, divorcee, financial difficulty,
marraige turmoil, children turmoil, family problems and other events. Let us learn
how to fly thru the storm. Either, we are going into a storm, are in a storm, or
just coming out of a storm. Let us say, " I can see the Sun thru the storm.

Take care of Jackie.

Your friend,

Roscoe

Roscoe Dixon

Roscoe Dixon was a highly respected
State Senator from Memphis who helped me
on mental health legislation & funding for m.h.
And he was my friend. He wrote this letter from
a federal penitentiary in Louisiana where he
served over two years (4?) for taking money illegally. (ours
He wrote back & forth while he was there. here
Letter now in a manze manilla envelop
in the house. He is a good man ! !
just sent him a note on his FaceBook
I hope to talk to him

88

For Jackie:

If you get an email from all your loved-ones in your address book in response to your Health Report your server will crash!!!

I am always in prayer for you and your health. Your faith and determination are an inspiration to everyone.

Sometimes I feel that our childhood and teen years spent together trump everyone else in the bond I have always felt we have. You may not fully realize the impact you had on my life as a child. I was truly weird when we met as young children, but you would have none of it, and forced me to overcome and lay aside the weirdness that had resulted from that early childhood loss. Mother's arrival, of course, had a huge impact on me, but a parent or step-parent can only do so much. I have long understood that your friendship in my early years allowed me to become who I am today and not the oddball misfit I would likely otherwise have become. We had such fun and you forced me into so many things I would otherwise either have avoided or not been permitted to do, and although I was never Olympic quality in learning to ride a bike, learning to swim or waterski, wasn't it all such fun!!! I truly felt I would never manage when your folks made the decision to move to Estill Springs. But the years of friendship, sharing and spiritual connection had built such a foundation of self confidence that as wrenching as it was for both of us, we prospered, reconnected at Lipscomb and as with the movie *The Way We Were*, I have often thought of that college period as "the best four years." This in the face of the decades of love, joy and peace we have both enjoyed with our own husbands, families and friends. And it also gave us the strength to weather the storms that accompany us in life. The separation, distance and demands of life never seemed to alter our connection allowing us to pick up and continue any time and any place.

I was delighted that we could have the "Golden Girl" period of friendship with both its pleasure and challenge!! Now that "we is all getting old" we don't buy green bananas, we puzzle at why our bodies have let us down, enjoy every sunrise, take naps, and praise the Lord for His goodness, mercy and grace. And the Lord was responsible for this blessing of such a special friendship which provided the groundwork for each of us to develop new and important friendships over the years. I treasure you and your huge tribe of a family and enjoy hearing about children, grands and great grands when they arrive!! I pray healing for your body and blessings on your body, mind and spirit. The Lord has you in His hand and will never leave you or forsake you. Such security provides the armour needed to defend against the miseries of life. Thank you for being you and being my friend! ⌐ t

Trish Hightower

Thanks, we got one. Trish your dear friend is beginning to die. For the most part she is comfortable with the help of her "babies" caring for her and the Hospice nurses. Her decline is slow but sure but can't say how much longer she will live. She knowa us and speaks a few words to us. I feel so blessed to have had her and to have had these years being so specially close while caring for her. She will die here at home with two windows looking out into her beautiful garden and all of us with her.
She has loved you since your days of childhood in Memphis where I fell in love with her. What a special friend you have been. Our love to you and George—George

She continues to be mostly comfortable with only occasional restlessness. I wish you could see our wonderful sons and daughter, their spouses and our grandchildren caring for her around the clock.They handle the morphine drops and our three giant sons lift her to the

commode and clean her. The Hospice worker bathed her yesterday. At times she rouses and talks a few words with them. Flowers from her garden are put fresh on the window sill right beside her every day. Brad's workers have planted all her new plants that she bought at two nurseies two weeks ago (she walked thro and made the selections herself).
She has said many wonderful and funny things. Lynch is keeping a running record of the days and nights. My sweet sister Jane is here part of every day giving support and hugs. And where would all be without Trina who is Jackie living on.
Thank you, thank you for your love and prayers and food and words. So many people love my beautiful, colorful, precious Jackie. I want you to know how much this means to us.
Her fine,fine nurse Valerie will be by again today and probably the pain medication will be increased a little.
We cry as I know many of you do but we are a strong family and have great love for each other--as Jackie set such an example for us.
Our granchildren are learning by watching and helping the importance of a good and loving life, without regrets and a love for God when death comes. We talk openly with them about what is happening and why. And you can see they are recieving their beloved "Baba's" last gift to them.
         Dear friends we love you--George

Hello George,

How very sad I am to hear that Jackie is not doing well. My memories are of a lovely, vivacious, funny, talented and good lady who appreciated everyone around her and encouraged them to be what they were no matter what that was. Only a few years older than me, Jackie taught me so much: how to survive pregnancy, how to manage growing boys, how to organize the grocery buying when one lives 40 minutes from Green Hills Grocery (God forbid), then cook, change diapers, keep the house tidy and entertain gatherings of no less than 12 people, and all with a large dose of humor. Jackie just seemed to have come here with all the information she needed. My memories run the gamut from floating down the Harpeth to picnics at Buggy Top Cave. From lucious dinners in your house on Shy's Hill Road to barbeques on Still House Hollow Road. I will always miss Jackie even though our paths haven't crossed often enough in the last few years. Both of your are very important and much respected influences in my "coming of age". Now, almost 49 years later we are saying good-bye. We just couldn't have visualized this time. I celebrate an extraordinary person and a life well lived. My love and wishes for peace and happiness to both of you.   Sandy

Subject: Jackie

This morning at 5:22 am, Jackie died peacefully as she took a few, soft, shallow breaths.
Brad, Lynch, Trina, Adam, Darwin and I were at her side touching and kissing her. Flowers from her garden were in small vases on the window sill beside her and the first calling of the morning birds just the otherside of the window.
Last night, there were grandchildren here going in and out, looking and patting on their "Baba"; then everyone was in the kitchen and dining and living room eating the good food people have brought, laughing, and telling "Baba" tales. On their own the grandchildren got a notebook and began to write page after page of short memories about their "tough", feisty, funny, teasing, beautiful, colorful, wise and loving grandmother.
How wonderful it has been having her here to die in her own home with her family and friends and Sally (our gentle chocolate Lab). Her surroundings have been filled with our tears and laughter and love. My how we
loved her!
Alive Hospice has guided and supported us all along. They are exceptional people--to all of them we send our "Thanks." We will follow up soon with information about the Memorial Service which we are hoping to have June 6, Saturday, in the afternoon.
My goodness, it is something how my wonderful Jackie has loved me all these years. My heart is broken but I tell you all, "My Lord it's been a party!" And can you imagine the party she's at now?

                              with all our love to all of you who love Jackie--
George

5/25/2009

Dear Friends,

I just wanted to let you all know that my mother passed away early

Monday morning. She died in her home with my father, my 4 brothers and

me by her side loving her all the way. Some of you know that she has

been battling cancer for almost 5 years. We did not expect death so

soon in the process, but in God's perfect wisdom and timing I now see

that this was the right time for her. She lived life more fully than anyone I have ever met, and up until the week before her death she was

in her yard cutting flowers, planting pots and living life. There will

be a huge void in our lives, but we are a strong close family and everything she taught us is in us so we know that we will go on being

strong and close. My mother was beautiful, fun loving, often a little

naughty, honest and fearless. She was one of a kind.

Both the visitation and memorial service will be held at Woodmont Hills

on June 6. Visitation will be from 1-3 and then the service will begin

at 3:00. The obituary will not run until Sunday.

I hope you are all well.

Much love,

Trina

Jackie Burton Spain

Nashville's 'Dead Eye Dora' Is Ready for Dove Season

January 16, 1936 • May 25, 2009

Saturday, June 6, 2009

Woodmont Hills Church of Christ

Memorial Service

Welcome~ **George Spain**

Prayer~ **John Davis**

Songs~ **Nick Boone**
   "O, Love That Wilt Not Let Me Go"
   "In Heavenly Love Abiding"

Psalm 91~ **Grandchildren**

Song~ **Grandchildren**
   "Down to the River to Pray"

Memories~ **Mr. Johnson**

Prayer~ **Mr. Johnson**

Memories with **George**

Photos with Music

Reflections~ **Lynch**

Reflections~ **Trina**

Song~ **Amy**

Reflections & Prayer~ **Mary** & **JoJo Brazil**

"I'll Fly Away"

"Baba's Dr. Pepper cup never leaves her side. It always has a lipstick ring around the straw." **Lillie**

"Me, Lillie and Jesse gave Baba a makeover at Estill and she sang opera to us. 'I'm so pretty...'" **Anna**

"Baba said the filter between her brain and her mouth was gone after surgery, but I think she just thought it was a funny excuse to say inappropriate things." **Leah**

"Once Baba drove all of the cousins in the back of her pickup truck to go swimming at Pickett State Park. It started raining though, and about nine of us tried to huddle under one beach towel. People we drove past were laughing their heads off, and I've always had a feeling Baba was one of them." **Jesse**

"I liked when I was playing basketball and the clock was running out and we were about to lose and my coach told me to hold the ball and wait until the game was over. Baba screamed out SHOOT IT! I looked at her and shook my head no." **Pearson**

"She let me play in her sink." **India**

"She was the best back scratcher." **Livia**

"I love Baba and I hug her and I love to go to her house to be with her and see her and I want her to be happy in heaven with God." **Zeke**

"When I came over for a sleepover, we made an outfit. It was a pink skirt with white lace and a tube top with lace straps." **Izzy**

"It was fun when Baba floored it when we were coming home from Estill." **Creed**

"Baba did flips with us into our pool." **Zoe**

"My favorite thing about her was that she did not judge people. I had a friend who recently met Baba. Many people would have thought he was a little sketchy because of the way that he dressed, but when he left Baba said, 'Well he seemed like a nice boy'". **Lealand**

"I remember Annie their dog was lying down sleeping and I tried to pet her. I startled her and she nipped me and I started crying. Grandma heard it and came right over with a small grin on her face as she tried not to laugh, but she took care of me at the same time." **Shane**

Jackie Burton Spain

SPAIN, Jackie Burton Age 73 of Nashville. May 25, 2009. Preceded in death by parents, Trinie and Nelson Burton. Survived by husband, George Spain; sons, Brad, Lynch, Adam and Darwin Spain; daughter, Trina Flynn; daughters-in-law, Sara, Angie and Lori Spain; son-in-law, Pat Flynn; grandchildren, Lealand, Livia, Anna, Jesse, Leah, Lillie, Pearson, Shane, Isabella, Creed, Zoe, India and Zeke; great grandchildren, Skyla and Hunter. Jackie lived life fearlessly and fully. She was an expert seamstress, gardener, state champion skeet shooter, great cook and decorator. She endeared herself to everyone with her kindness, grace and naughty sense of humor. She appreciated everyone around her and encouraged all to be what they were no matter what that was. She loved her family, friends and God with all her heart. Friends are cordially invited to a visitation with the family from one o'clock in the afternoon until three o'clock on Saturday, the 6th of June at Woodmont Hills Church of Christ. A memorial service will be conducted at three o'clock on Saturday following the visitation at Woodmont Hills Church of Christ. The Spain family has requested that anyone attending the services wear colorful clothing in memory of Mrs. Spain. Thank you Alive Hospice for your gentle Christian Care. In lieu of flowers, memorial contributions in memory of Mrs. Spain may be directed to Vanderbilt-Ingram Cancer Center, Clinical Trial Research, Care of gift processing, PMB407727, 2301 Vanderbilt Pl., Nashville, TN 37240; Alive Hospice, Inc., 1718 Patterson Street, Nashville TN 37203 or David Lipscomb-Development, 1 University Park Dr., Nashville, TN 37204. WOODLAWN-ROESCH-PATTON FUNERAL HOME, (615) 383-4754

Thank you for coming to this remembrance of our
beautiful, colorful, gifted, funny, wise and loving Jackie
adventuresom.
- our Baba - who treated everyone the same - with
kindness and respect.

Thank you for the love & support you have given Jackie & our family

Special thanks to :
Her brothers & their wives Nelson & Ann Burton & A.M. & Martha Burton
My sister Jane Myers
All the doctors & nurses at Vanderbilt & Baptist & private physicians,
    and the good-kind valet parkers at Vanderbilt
Alive Hospice nurses
Woodlawn Cemetary & Woodmont Hills Ch. of Christ
Our neighbors
Steve Brumfield
All the musicians , Pat, Amy .
Our friends & extended family

Our grandchildren who sat with her and loved on her .

No children could have taken better care of their mother
in her last days & hours than did : Brad & Lynch & Trina, Adam &
Darwin & their spouses .

Not long before Jackie died Lillie - one of our grandchildren wrote
"Baba calls Papa, Bubbas and he calls her Babes,
They are madly in love."

George at Jackie's Memorial
6/6/09

98

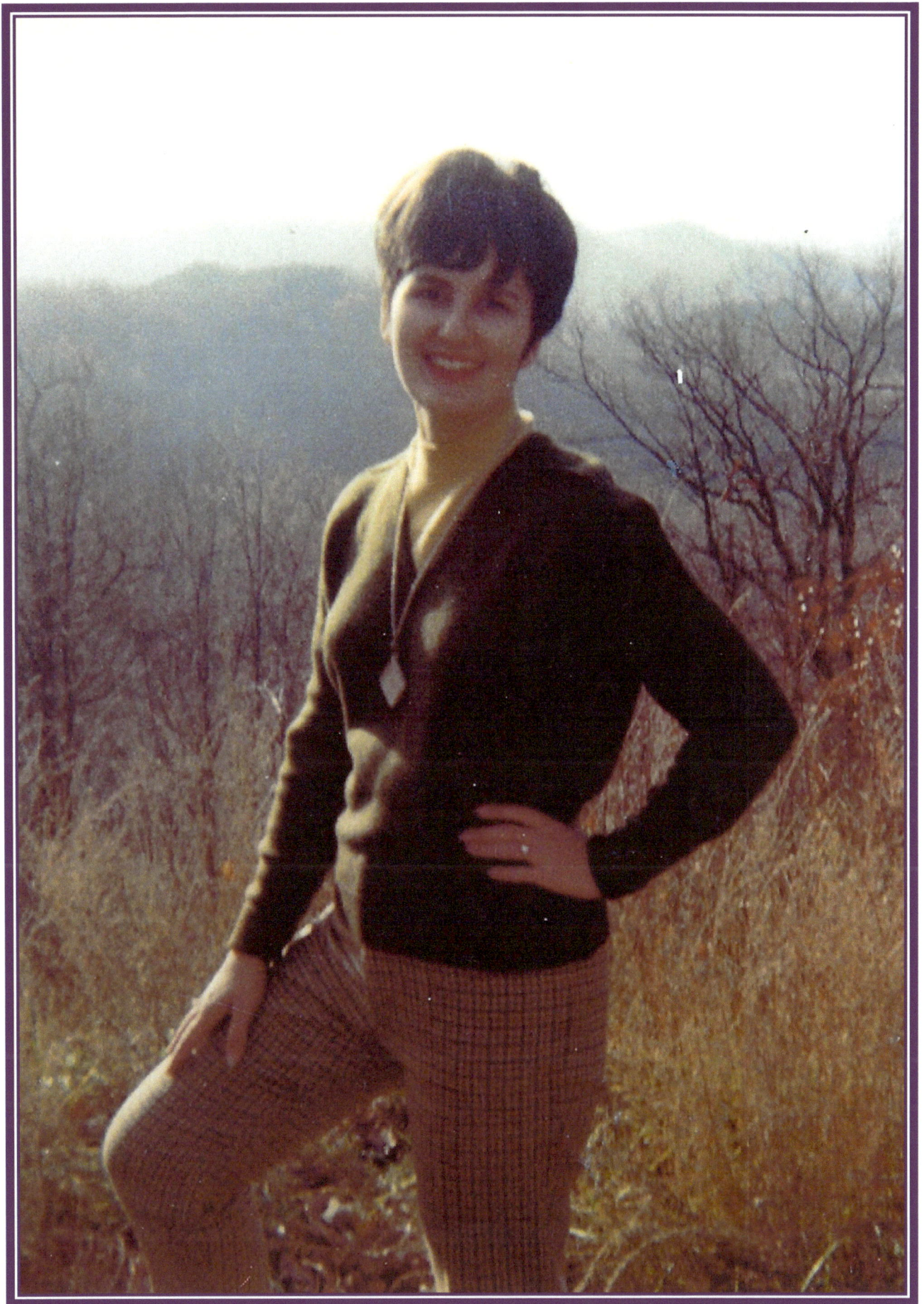

JoJo and I would like to thank George and his children for giving us the opportunity to share with you some of the thoughts and emotions that we, like many of you, are experiencing on this day which has been set aside to remember and celebrate the awesome life and legacy of our beloved Jackie Burton Spain.

My first awareness that there was a Jackie Burton began one September afternoon in 1954 when Nicky Boone and I were chatting in my living room on Woodmont Blvd, which was about a mile from the Lipscomb campus. George Edward, that's what I called him since we had begun the first grade together when everyone had a double name. George Edward came bursting in the front door with the exclaimation, "Boone, what in the world are you doing here? All of the guys are over at Johnson Hall helping the freshmen girls move into the dorm. And man, you won't BELIEVE one of the girls who's come up from Winchester...her name is Jackie Burton, A.M. Burton's grand-daughter, and she is gorgeous!!"

Well, it didn't take Nicky long to act on that little piece of information. He had a date with Jackie to go to the Tennessee State Fair, which was always in the middle of September back then. So, the gang went with Nicky and Jackie on their first date. I can tell you this, all eyes were on Jackie Burton, the new girl in town. I think Nick and Jackie dated off and on for about a year, because if my memory serves me correctly it was the Labor Day of 1955 that I was spending the week-end with Jackie and her parents down in Estill Springs when the two George Edwards...Spain and Brazil...came down to go and water ski, on the lake, which was adjacent to the Burton home. Mr. and Mrs. Burton treated us to steaks that night and it was a very memorable occasion. I really don't remember whether Nicky and Jackie were still dating at all, however, I do remember that George and Jackie very soon became an item and were the talk of the campus.   Fast Forward about 18 months..

I was privileged to be asked to be in Jackie and George's wedding and thus began a foursome friendship that has lasted some 55 years.

I would like to build my thoughts today, using words which begin with the letters of her name: J>A>C>K>I and E.

J: Even though many words beginning with this letter come to mind: jovial, jolly, jubilant, jaunty, I have chosen the word JOY. Jackie's "joy for and of life" came from her relationships. First, was her relationship with Jesus Christ. This association with Christ and The Father enabled Jackie to weather the storms of life, through which all of us must travel. Her faith never waivered and her life was a testimony to that faith.

Second, was the wonderful relationship with her family, which has already been described to you by her husband and children. And thirdly, her relationships with her friends, which was evidenced by the many, many times we, and others, were entertained in their homes. She hosted anywhere from small dinner parties to

Fourth of July celebrations which several times reached over a hundred people.

A: We could chose amiable, which she was, appealing, which she was, or, as her husband mentioned, adventuresome: she loved water skiing, was a champion skeet shooter, traveled the Amazon, climbed the hills of Scotland and loved horse back riding...or mule riding, which ever animal was close at hand.

However, I would like to use the words: AVAILABLE and ATTENTIVE:

Jackie was available to spend time with her friends. She recognized, and was attentive to, their needs. Sandy Zeigler, who was a close friend of Jackie's, as were so many of us, said it so well in a note written to George a couple of days before Jackie left us. Sandy agreed to allow me to share some of her words with you today. She writes:
"Only a few years older than me, Jackie taught me so much: how to survive pregnancy, how to manage growing boys,

how to organize the grocery buying when one lives 40 minutes from Green Hills Grocery (God forbid), then cook, change diapers, keep the house tidy and entertain gatherings of no less than 12 people, and all with a large dose of humor. Jackie just seemed to have come here with all the information she needed."

I, personally, can recall at least three instances in my life when I was going through some unusually tumultuous and troubling times. All it took was a phone call to Jackie and she was beside me in thirty minutes: comforting, consoling and praying with, and for, me.

Which brings me to our third letter:

C: Caring, calm and composed under pressure. All of this when others might have lost their cool. Jackie was noted for her charisma and cleverness. However, I feel that most of all of these "C" words, Jackie was _capable_ and _competent._ This competency and capability was shown in the exemplary fashion in which she transformed the five places in which the Spains lived into perfectly beautiful HOMES. If my memory serves me correctly, their first home was in a small apartment on Bernard Circle, near the Belmont campus. The second was in a duplex on Maplehurst. Third, was a house on Shy's Hill. Fourth, the spacious country estate on Still House Hollow Road in Williamson County and finally the very comfortable, family centered house on North Observatory Drive. All of these dwellings, from small apartments to large houses ...were just that: DWELLINGS...Jackie transformed them into beautiful HOMES. And I'm going to fudge a little bit here and use this as a segway into: Our fourth letter:

K: Because of Jackie's knack for the unusual and "know-how" with the sewing machine, she had the ability to make the curtains, bedspreads, pillow shams, table cloths, napkins, and yes, even Christmas decorations to adorn these beautiful homes. Since Jackie became the QUEEN of all h homes, I was tempted to use her formal name, Jacquelyn, but then I would have had to come up with some "U"s which I did: Utterly Unique. But, I digress, and my children have all warned me not to become too lengthy.

However, we can't leave "K" without honoring Jackie's KINDNESS. And this was a kindness shown to ALL people, whether they were really good friends, or those she barely knew. She had a gentleness and kindness about her persona which has been brought to my attention by several people when we were speaking of Jackie. You see, she and George shared these beautiful homes with many people...many times. No one was unimportant to Jackie. Every one was worthy of her time and attention.

I: Our Jackie was a person of unsurpassed and unquestioned INTEGRITY.

E: Example >>>> Jackie has left us with many good examples of how to live a full and fruitful life. She also has left us with a more DIFFICULT example: How to die, with grace and dignity....full of courage and a surety of her eternal destination.

Anyone listening to the words I have had to say in the last several minutes would think, if you did not know her well, that I was speaking some PERFECT person...one who made no mistakes. One who never did, or said, anything that was not "JUST RIGHT". Jackie was, like us all,...human. Naturally, since I loved her so much, I didn't see her weaker traits, and if I did, I'm surely not going to tell you about them today. Now, SHE would tell you about them.. that goes back up to her integrity.

I think she would also tell you this: Live each day to the fullest. Love God, your family and your friends and never, ever, take each other for granted. Jackie, we sure are going to miss you, girl......

Mary Brazil

SEE YOU AT THE HOUSE

WE ARE GATHERED HERE TODAY

TO LAUGH AND CRY AND CELLEBRATE A WOMAN

MOTHER, BABA, LOVING WIFE

THAT GIRL SURE COULD SPICE UP LIFE...FOR EVERYONE

NOTHING LIKE THAT SOUTHERN DRAWL

WRAPPING LOVE AROUND US ALL

THROWING PARTIES, THROWING SHOES,

CATCHING UP ON ALL THE NEWS

SAYING SHE TOOK ALL THE STRAGGLERS IN,

MADE THEM FEEL LIKE FRIENDS...SAYING

SEE YOU AT THE HOUSE, EVERYBODY'S WAITING

SUPPERS ON THE TABLE, THE SUN IS SLOWLY FADING

FLOWERS FILL HER GARDEN, SOMEWHERE MUSIC'S PLAYING

CHILDREN IN THE YARD, FEELS SO GOOD WE'RE STAYING

SEE YOU AT THE HOUSE

SOME FOLKS HAVE A NATURAL GIFT

TO BE AT EASE IN ANY SITUATION

SHE NEVER MADE YOU WAIT HER OUT

TO FIND OUT WHAT SHE THOUGHT ABOUT...OR WHO SHE WAS

THE ONE-EYED JACK, THE BEAUTY QUEEN,

SHE FOUND GOOD IN EVERYTHING

SHE MADE YOU LAUGH, SHE MADE YOU THINK

CALL IT HOPE, CALL IT FAITH, I LOOK FORWARD TO THE DAY

WE'LL ALL HEAR JACKIE SAY...

SEE YOU AT THE HOUSE, EVERYBODY'S WAITING

SUPPER'S ON THE TABLE, AND THE SUN IS NEVER FADING

AND THAT OLD FAMILIAR FEELING...SWEET ANTICIPATION

OF FINALLY COMING HOME

AND THIS TIME WE'LL BE STAYING.

SEE YOU AT THE HOUSE.

WRITTEN AND SUNG BY AMY GRANT GILL AT JACKIE'S MEMORIAL

Hi Everybody,

I was at Daddy's today and he said that he wants to go ahead and take some of Mama's ashes to Estill on Father's Day since everyone will be there. There are several places that he wants to sprinkle them. It seems like it will be a nice time to do that.

We are going to get barbeque for everyone and then people can reimburse Daddy for what their family eats. We can figure an approximate amount or we can just wing it.

I've talked to Martha and Ann and rather that designating certain things for people to bring they suggested just making it pot luck. Adam said that he will make some beans, Sara will bring a watermelon and some other fruit (grapes), I'll make some potato salad and maybe that broccoli salad stuff. Darwin and Lori just bring whatever you want to. Darwin those eggs in the shells were delicious and so much fun for everyone to peel. They were a food and an activity all rolled into one! There are a lot of waters and leftover drinks that people brought to Daddy's house so I think that we will be doing ok on drinks.

I guess just shoot for getting there at least by noon if you can. Mark Burton will be bringing a boat and hopefully Daniel will too if he comes. It will be a fun day.

See you all on Sunday, 8-)

Trina

110

Sent: Sunday, June 21, 2009 6:58 PM
Subject: Father's Day

What a day, with a large gathering of our family: children, grandchildren, cousins, inlaws, etc. We scattered some of Jackie's ashes on Elk River in front of her home, and some in the yard around the great pear tree, and on special plants from the mountain, and some under the

children's swing, and some on the cheap faded, pink, plastic flamingoes.
The children sang "Down to the River to Pray" led by that sweet little India. They were standing on the lower deck only a few feet from the water.
There was swimming and boating and the telling of tales and laughing and hugging and eating for hours. IT WAS WONDERFUL! Jackie would have loved it (but of course she would have thought it a bit overdone, and of course it would have been if she hadn't been worth every bit of it).
What a wonderful Father's Day. I send the same from us to all of you--George

Sent: Friday, November 13, 2009 8:04 AM
Subject: Re: Painter and Faulkner

Sounds like you all had a fun day.   Mine had many tears as I went thro thousands of photos in thirty plus large albums locating pictures related to stories we will tell Sunday pm in the three hour filming. Jackie made most of them: of our children, grchildren, friends and adventures: hiking in Wales, Amazon River, Devil's Island, canoing on Rio Grand into Mexico, white water rafting, rappeling, hunting in Mexico, climbing remote Mayan and Aztec temples, camping with over a hundred Sioux for a week on Wounded Knee battlefield for the Sundance, Hudson Bay, Germany for Xmas, Prague, England, riding horseback in Copper Canyon, riding on a train with bullet holes from bandits that held it up the month before, the Xmas Jam, riding for seventeen years with our family in Big South Fork, hiking into Lost Cove and to Buggytop Cave, Estill Springs Seaside, Mesa Verde, Chaco Canyon, Telluride, Glacier National Park, our exciting years living in a semi-wild forest among whiskey makers, cock fighters, killers-riding, hunting, milking, falconry, canoing, gardening, swimming, snakes and dogs, pigs and chickens and on and on--my Lord what a wonderful life we have had, but most of all our five children, thirteen grchildren, two gr-grchildren, and my special sister Jane and our dear, dear friends -"The Herd." WHAT A LIFE!--George

Our good freiend, Jerry Henderson from our college days at Lipscomb, said these words about Jackie a few days ago and, at my request, he wrote them down for me to share with you. As those of you who knew her well know Jackie was a special gift to us all--and I miss her so, oh Lord do I miss her--George

George...
this is the essence of what I said. It was spontaneous at the time, but I had said the same thing to many of our friends before...

Jerry

Jackie's not being in our midst has certainly made us all think of lots of qualities about this beautiful person.

Jackie was the most secure and self-sufficient person I've ever known. I'm sure most of this was innate but I'm also sure that her wonderful parents allowed her to extend herself to make all that happen.

I knew she was secure because she could do virtually 'anything'. Not only could she 'do' anything, but usually she could do it better than anyone else. The amazing thing about her, though, was that she didn't display this, it was just merely true. She never made anyone else feel insecure because they couldn't do it as well as she.

Looking back, I realize that, in any discussion among our group, Jackie was always saying exactly what she felt, never felt in any way intimidated even if she was the only one thinking a certain way. BUT, I also noticed that almost everyone accepted her 'way' when it was over, because it was usually the 'best way'. She just seemed to see things more clearly and was able to draw conclusions without prejudice. And she never seemed aggressive in insisting that anyone agree with her. Of course I didn't see her in all situations, but I never saw her angry; she was always so very understanding of others views;...she just had an incredible spirit of love.

I personally miss her very much and still have great difficulty imagining her not among us.

New Year's Eve
With the Herd
A Toast To Our Jackie

When I started having our New Year's Eve Party, it was because our Jackie could no longer host the event. She was the New Year's Eve Queen, and I never tried to 'cover' what she did for so many years.

This year I want to host the party to honor Jackie. She was a friend to all of us, and I well remember the parties in Liepers Fork and in Nashville, as well as her wonderful smile and willingness to get us all together.

This year, please be at the Davis home at 6:00. At 6:15 we will have our toast to Jackie and tell a short something that we remember about her. Also we will have appetizers' with our Champagne.

Around 7:00 we will share a light supper. I am hopeful all of you will be in attendance.

This is what each of you should bring:

Brazils & Boones, Broccoli Salad
Johnsons & Hendersons, Strawberry Salad
Davys & George and Jane, Ramen Noodle Salad
Jennings, Arnold & Haileys, Appetizers'
Davis's, Ham & Cheese Sandwiches & Dessert

I still have plenty of champagnes from the last couple of years. Don't bring more. If you wish to have a particular wine for supper, you may bring this.

For those who need recipes, I have them.

Jayne and John

Sent: Tuesday, January 12, 2010 7:33 PM
Subject: Story for Jan. 16

Picture this. Its about 1961 and Zig and I are enjoying dinner at George and Jackie's house on Shy's Hill Road. There are probably more people there but I don't recall who.
At any rate, Jackie at her methodical and wordy best launches into some current information which she thinks we'll find interesting.

She says a guy has come to mow and she asks him if he has any idea why the grass is dead and brown in spots just off the back terrace.
"Yeah", he says, "it looks like where your dog is going."
"But", she says, "we don't have a dog." Snickers are heard in the audience.
 "Now Jackie...." George is oddly becoming ill at ease.
"No, let me finish", Jackie pushes on. "So I thought, Aha, George goes outside and wanders around every night. So *that's* what he's doin'!
Everyone is shrieking with laughter. Everyone, that is, except George.
 "Now Jackie....," says George.
Jackie impishly continues, "Not only that but the other night I was awakened by something thrashing around in the bedroom draperies! Just as I thought I was goin' to have to get up and get my gun, I heard moaning".
 "Now Jackie..."
"It was George!" she exclaims. "He couldn't find the bathroom in the dark, went the opposite way and got hung up in the draperies."
Everyone, especially me, is howling with tears rolling down our faces. I am especially guilty.

George is not amused and remains a little distant the rest of the evening. He is only around 25 years old and probably finds it difficult to see anything amusing about making public his bathroom problems.

This is probably a had-to-be-there-story, however, those who knew Jackie well often enjoyed her ability to weave a story into a hilarious tapestry. Of course, this had a more elaborate build up than I can possibly reconstruct which only served to make it funnier. Jackie never shied away from vividly pointing out any of George's unique behaviors.

Sandy Ziegler

113

August 14, 2009

Mr. George E. Spain
1724 N. Observatory Drive
Nashville, TN 37215

Dear George:

I am so touched by the gift of the First Edition of Gabriel Garcia Marquez'
One Hundred Years of Solitude to Beaman Library. We rarely receive gifts of
rare books, and for dedicated book lovers, this is a treasure. As director of this
library, I appreciate also the fact that gifts such as these enhance the value of our
collection substantially and are valuable for our students and faculty as primary
resources. I am at a loss for words to convey our gratitude.

Saying all of this, the foremost reason I personally find this gift so meaningful is
that you chose something that you valued to give to us in memory of your beloved
Jackie. I understand that so well. Jackie's legacy is already somewhat enshrined
in this institution through her family, but this emphasizes the qualities that make
both of you so very special- the love of beauty, of God's natural world, of the
commitment to the written word, of family, and surely not the least of these, your
love for your Lord.

We are placing this book in our Special Collections, which does not mean it won't
be used, only that it is restricted use because of its value. We will use it for displays,
for promotional purposes, and anyone doing research in early editions will surely
find it valuable. Once we place the record in WorldCat, the fact we have this goes
all over the world.

I value the gift of friendship you and Jackie always extended to me, and one that
you continue to offer. I cherish the memory of Jackie as a beautiful free spirit whose
life inspired us all.

Warmest regards,

Carolyn T. Wilson
Director
Beaman Library

February 4, 2010

Mr. George E. Spain and family
1724 N. Observatory Dr.
Nashville, TN 37215

Dear George and family:

We don't often receive gifts of rare books as nice or as valuable as your gift of a first edition of Gabriel Garcia Marquez' *One Hundred Years of Solitude.* We are honored that you are entrusting our library with this wonderful gift. As I explained to you, gifts coming into the library valued at $5000 or over, must have an independent appraisal by an antiquarian dealer, and since you have that, you are well in compliance with IRS requirements when you file this gift.

 We also understand the gift is given in memory of Jacqueline Burton Spain (you might let me know if you prefer the formal Jacqueline or just Jackie for the bookplate) and that it is given by you and your children, Brad, Lynch, Trina Flynn, Adam and Darwin. All of this will appear on our bookplates, which will be in the book in accordance with guidelines for materials housed in our Special Collections.

All of us who knew and admired and loved Jackie will never forget her. But after you and I go to join our mates, there will be a legacy here in her name that will benefit researchers, scholars, students and faculty for years in the future. It is indeed a permanent memorial and an appropriate one. We thank you and your family profoundly for making us the recipient of this gift.

Warmest regards,

Carolyn T. Wilson
Director
Beaman Library

115

TAKING GOO GOOS TO THE SIOUX

By George Spain

Twenty years ago my wife, our oldest son, and his girlfriend and I spent a week camping with the Sioux on the Pine Ridge Sioux Reservation, in South Dakota. Because our son had taken a large truck filled with winter clothing as a gift to the Sioux we were invited by Zac Bear Shield, a medicine man, to come to the Sun Dance, a traditional religious ceremony where the dancers have their flesh pierced as a spiritual offering. The dance was held on part of the Wounded Knee Battlefield with guards, a mile away at the road entrance, to prevent anyone entering who had not been invited. Our two tents were set up near the circular dance grounds and next to the tents and teepees of over one hundred Sioux.

My wife, Jackie, a soft-voiced, Scarlett O'Hara-southern beauty, had the inspired idea of taking a case of Goo Goos with us. It was the first time the Sioux had eaten that perfect mixture of chocolate, caramel, marshmallow and roasted peanuts. Goo Goos were an instant hit! At rest periods during the day children would rush to our tent and push and shove one another to get one. But Jackie, who was as firm about good manners as she was beautiful, would stop them with, "Ya'll quit that now, be polite and ask, 'Can I have a Goo Goo, pleeease?'" When they did, she would give them one. Later we overheard some children mimicking her, "Ya'll may I pleeease have a Goo Goo, pleeease Ya'll!"

At night, Indians would come and sit around our fire, drink coffee, eat Goo Goos and tell about their lives and about their ancestors who were traveling on the "Spirit Road" of stars in the sky.

Today at Pine Ridge, I am sure there are Indians who remember the pretty soft-voiced lady from Tennessee who fed them the most delicious candy they had ever eaten and perhaps still say, "Goo Goo pleeease" for candy.

116

Journals

Written by: Lynch, Sara, and Jesse Spain
Typed by: Anna Spain

- Parker Smith's brother said Mama was the best water skier on the river a great athlete and shot

- Ben Lynch favorite cousin and had a crush on her as a little boy

Lynch

Mama always refers to us as "Precious" always calling for "Bubbas". Daddy is the only one to calm Mama.

5-20-09 early morning

Heard Daddy in the bathroom and thought it was someone at the door. She yelled "come". Mama sounded just like Trinie.

Adam and I stayed. How has Daddy done this? <u>Love</u>

Brad came by and sat with Mama a while and has gone to Franklin but will be back. Leah got in last night. She slept with the dog and it peed on the bed, or so she says, and they'll be on soon.

Adam has gone after Angie and Sara and the girls will be on the road soon.

10 a.m.

Daddy is sitting with Mama and I'm watching the phone. Soon the nurse will call and be by. I hope Trina comes on soon. Mama's breathing is labored. I don't know what to do.

10 a.m. Mama, Daddy, Lynch.

Jane is here everyday I guess. She'll take care of us all. Mrs. Brazil just called. She said they'll come by this afternoon. Everybody, we're all real sad but Heaven will be so much prettier. Soon Mama will be tending the gardens of Heaven.

10:08

Trina is here. Daddy has noticed and commented on breathing. Trina is having Leah come on.

11:00

Nelson and Ann are here. Mama lifted her arm by herself to hug Ann. Ann said how when Mama was a girl she loved to lay her head in Ann's lap and have her back tickled.

11:22

Matt and Daniel Burton are here. Mama tells everyone how precious they are and that's how she always treated us all.

11:37

Nelson and Leah are here. Mama started crying and put her arm around Leah saying "My precious, my big eyed girl". This made her so happy.

11:50

Trina came back with Lillie while they were hugging Mama said "she needs a tissue"

12:21

Angie is here with Adam

1:02

Brazils came first at 1:16 they went in to see Mama. Nurse came at 1 p.m. and helped us in moving. She calmed Mama that she was there at our birth and will wait for us in our rebirth.

118

Becky, Monica, and her boy.
>1:17

From the nurse we are in a final time.
>1:53

Pat and Pearson are here, Lori came also. Jane is keeping all straight with the nurse. Around 1:30 we got Mama on toilet. We sat her back on bed. She passed gas and said "poot".
>2:00

Nurse is talking about seeing things "Mothers, angels, etc." she said they see different things. Mama will see wonderful things from Heaven I think. Trina and nurse say we need to help Daddy rest. It's on in the afternoon. Mama has been resting. She was nervous but Daddy got her calmed down as he does.
>3:45 or so

Sara, Anna, and Jesse arrived. They've taken turns sitting.
Its been decided that 2 weeks after we'll have a memorial service.
>Around 6 p.m.

Trina and I got the patch on. Mama forgot where she was she said I keep forgetting. Even now Mama is a comfort as she was 48 years ago till this day. The girls and Sara spoke with Mama.
Lou and Beth Saggio came by she told Beth she was precious. Right now they are looking at pictures. They love Mama so.

Jesse
>At dark

She wants Bubbas. She doesn't like the morphine. When she coughs it sounds strange but no one does anything. Daddy's telling her about the flowers. I'm not sure she understands. I'll tell her I love her, despite the fact she might not know I'm here, or I'm me. I'll go. She has to use the portable toilet.

Lynch
>10:? p.m.

Trina, Adam, and myself are sitting up with Mama. Daddy is sleeping. He's so tired. Sara and Angie are in the kitchen visiting. Mama's head is turned looking towards Trina. This is very much like with Trinie, a daughter caring for her Mama.
Mama was calling for me to hold her hand. She was a bit frustrated. Adam figured it out that Mama had to tinkle cause she went "1,2,3". Adam got her up and later Trina cleaned her with a rag. Angie is sitting with Mama. This night of sitting will be long. Mama called for Trina. They share words and thoughts only mothers and daughters can share. We were talking about Pearson and myself being lefties. It went on to all Pearson.

>**5-21-09** 4:15

Mama complained twice saying she hurt. The second time that her legs hurt. She has been saying that "everyone got ham Bubbas". Always she calls for Daddy. She just asked Trina if the ham was good. "Was the ham good?". Trina described the cut and the type of rolls. Only they understood that. We gave Mama some morphine. She was a bit sick but we took care of her. Mama and Trina's conversation is very clear. Daddy slept through the night. Watching those brief moments that I'm in the room when Daddy is holding Mama's hand and comforting her is like the countless observations through my life. Daddy is so devoted to my Mama and loves her so. We all do, but not like Daddy. Trina called the nurse. Mama said she hurt. Again she mentioned ham so maybe it was a recurring thought. Mama apologized for being sick. I told her of the example she has set as a mother and a Christian person and how strong she has always been through our life.

> 5:30 or so

Shortly I'll wake Daddy. Maybe 6:30 or 7

> 6:02

Mama took some more morphine. She is still strong. She stood up earlier after tinkling. She told Sara, Trina, and myself "Am I dying?" Trina asked if she wanted to and Mama said no. We both told her to go when she and God are ready.

Trina told Mama we would take her out to see her flowers if she wanted. That would be nice. Her eyes got so big yesterday when Adam brought in some he gathered from her garden.

Yesterday seems likes years ago. I was so unsure and scared. I think Adam was too. So quickly we have all fallen into a natural role that has no fear. She is aware of who is here. I was coughing, sitting in Daddy's chair. Mama said "Lynch is coughing" They've propped her feet up. Trina has raised the blind so Mama can see outside. I do know the connection between Mama, us, her home, Sally and the garden is strong.

Mama is taking some big sips from Slim Fast. Sara and Trina are helping. Sara told her of her clippings and that they took root. Mama said "good" in that Mama voice.

Sara was leaning on the oxygen tube and said that would be bad if it was cut off. Mama smiled and Trina said "Sara will write this down later"

> 12 noon

The Davis came by Mama had been talking to me.

Now she is hugging the Darwin's bunch. They had sung a song to Mama many kisses and a hug then a picture. Mama's good eye opened wide. This all wore her out. She's tired and stomach hurts. Now we'll relax. Mama said "I feel bad" I wish I could help her. Adam has sure taken care of Mama. He's so good with her. Much like Mama.

Sara

> Early afternoon

The Boone's are here and Brad ahs taken the children (Livia, Anna, Jesse, Leah) who were here out for popsicles. You are resting so peacefully so I trust you don't feel pain. I don't want you to hurt. I'm remembering all the things that have gone on in this very room where you are resting. The very first time Lynch brought me over to meet ya'll, you were sitting in the exact same spot where you now lie. George was in the recliner. Anna and Leah as toddlers watching cartoons and Disney. Babies taking steps for the first time. Waiting to eat a holiday meal and smelling the rolls finish baking. All this and so much more. Oh yes, and curling up on the couch as Sally nudged to get up close to you. (And Annie and Pumpkin!) Thank you for always listening. No matter what you were doing, you answered the phone and listened as if you'd been waiting for our call. You've been a good multitasker. You probably were gardening, cleaning, cooking, etc. while we were talking. George just peeked in to check on you. You are still sleeping, so he is visiting with the Boone's. They brought you a red rose in a vase and sat it on the window ledge so you can see it when you wake up.

Lynch

Around 3 probably 3:30

Mama has had a bath. This lady was the first nurse I've seen tear up. Mama affects people in this way. The Boone's came by. Mama had said she wanted to see them and no others but of course she did. Nelson and Ann came by. Nelson has his holster on but left the pistol in the car. Now Mama and Daddy sit. Daddy tells Mama how beautiful she is, of her garden, and of her children which come directly after Daddy. He asks to kiss her and she says yes. After they stare at each other as only they can.

3:54

Watching Trina with Mama is so much like Mama and Trinie.

God is with us.

Many e-mails and letters are read. They all say the same things. Either Mama, but usually Mama and Daddy always made them feel special and opened their home to them. Mama is resting.

Last night Trina said "Mama if I could take this on myself I would in a second". I've said those same words. How many times have we all said those same words? We love Mama and Daddy so we would give them our lives for which is no less than they would do for us.

Sara

5-21 early evening

You're sound asleep, and Lynch is sitting next to you. I'm hoping you'll wake up but know you need to rest now. I wonder if you can hear the sounds of the ocean on the sound machine that's been running 24/7 since Tuesday. I'm thinking of the song "On Jordan's Stormy Banks" "I stand and cast a wishful eye. To Canaan's fair and happy land where my possessions lie. We will rest in the fair and happy land by and by just across on the ever green shore, sing the song of Moses and the lamb by and by, and dwell with Jesus ever more." Won't that be something when we all are together again with no cancer, no pain, no tears, no worries. I can't wait for you to meet my mother and grandmother. They had many of those good southern traits that you have, but most of all, they loved God, just as you do. We're all related, because we are all his children.

I was walking through your garden earlier and wishing I had asked you the names of all those flowers and plants. I want to have a pretty garden like yours when we get into our house.

Lynch

After 9 p.m.

Anna helped me move Mama up so she could drink. She was afraid she would throw up. Sara watched and held the drink. Anna is strong. Trina will stay to help Adam and myself. She was going to go but Mama asked her to stay. Trina is asking Mama what her favorite flower is. She said Johnson grass and laughed. "Sara fix my feet" Trina mentioned "we are all around like a bunch of chicks." We said a prayer..

Now I lay me down to sleep, I pray the Lord my soul to keep. If I should die before I wake, I pray the Lord my soul to take. God bless Mama and Daddy and Brad, Lynch, Trina, Adam, and Darwin and all the little babies.

We got her up to tinkle.

5-22-09 6:30 a.m.

Mama slept through the night but woke at 4:30 or so in pain. I came in. Adam who had been up was of course taking care of Mama. We will get the nurse Valerie to ask questions we have on giving Mama more comfort as this changes.

Daddy slept the night. Around 6:15 we gave Mama a suppository. The first was last night. I rolled her towards me and of course she had a smile because Darwin and Trina drew a ticket. This helps with the throwing up. Today we organize more specific jobs for others. Brad keeps Mama's garden beautiful and brings much garden stuff. The garden is so important and before coming down worried. He will keep her pride and joy beautiful.

8:35 a.m.

The suppository makes Mama so tired. All seem relatively clear when there was a level of recognition. Now I'm scared. Trina was crying and said she was scared Mama would not recognize her. I had the same fear and fear that maybe all is wrong. It's not though, all is right. We all die. I whispered in Mama's ear "I love you" she responded "I love you too". She is still and always will be with us. Death, drugs, nor coma can separate us. We cannot separate ourselves form Mama because of who and what she has always been to us.

9:30 or so a.m.

Mama's eyes are partly open mere slivers. Her breathing seems different. All of my thoughts lead to crying. Just then I couldn't remember the last time she hugged me. When I cry I put her hand to my face. It calms me and makes me feel safe.

10 or 11 am

We are taking pictures not stage just us and Mama. Michele is here with Macy. The flowers in the window grow. Not from a store like someone would buy, arranged for the masses, but single flowers from her garden. There is one brought by the Boones. It has 2 blooms and 2 that will bloom. One each for Nick and Trish and each for Mama and Daddy.

She is so beautiful.

About 12 noon

The filter to the oxygen has been fixed. Brad is here and got Mama another blanket and has fixed her up. Lori Hamilton has gone for meds. They are giving us another patch which will help. Trina has gone to work for just a bit. Adam and Angie have left for Krogers. Adam was kicked out for questioning why they had a communist China flag in the store. He'll bring back a story I'm sure. Daddy sits reading with one hand resting on Mama. Her breathing is different and her legs restless.

When you say "it seems a lifetime these past days" it's true. All things we were taught by our folks are coming into play at each moment of our existence in this house.

1:00 p.m.

Mama was groaning and Lori got back when it started. As the Brazils walked down the drive Mama had to tinkle. She pooed and egg (guinea) and a bit of diarrhea she spoiled her gown a bit. What little we did weakened her quite a bit. Brad wiped her and Daddy found a beautiful colored Mexican gown. We dressed her and gave her some oxycodone which did not make her sick then go on the patch.

Mama's responses are small. She does hear us though. The meds and her current state have caused such weakness. I need to speak with Adam about catheter.

2:30 p.m.

Bernie Arnold has come to said bye to Mama. Her husband and she were close friends. They met in school at Lipscomb. He was a WWII paratrooper. A fine man with a fine wife.

Bernie whispered to Mama and she recognized opening her eyes and lifting her head slowly.

Sara

Early evening

Anna just now walked in quietly, and without hesitation, George got up and gave her his seat next to Jackie. I do believe that's the best gift he's ever given her-a portion of the little time he has left with his wife, he is sharing with Anna. What a sacrifice of love. As I look at them, I am remembering my first baby, Anna, as we prepared to move to South Dakota. Jackie insisted on going with us to help drive and then stayed for nearly a week helping to scrub and clean the kitchen, She probably scrubbed that nasty refrigerator for two hours or more, while I took a nap. She helped me scrub the cabinets and figure out where to put everything. I remember that she made a list of all the things she knew I would need (Drano, sink screen, etc.) so when we went to Rapid City we had a list. She said the first thing she always did when she moved into a new house was pour Drano down the sinks. Before she went home, she suggested propping Anna up in her big stroller and rolling her around the house as I did things so she could see what was going on. Now we've come full circle as we attempted to elevate the bed and position Jackie to be more comfortable.

Jackie, thank you so much for loving my girls. Thank you for loving me. Thank you for sending Jesse the spending money for her Washington trip. She bought a souvenir at the Smithsonian for ya'll, so she'll share it with George. I can just hear you saying "Oh-h-h...I be you had the best ti-i-ime!" And then you would listen to all the details. You're such a part of George, "the blood of his heart", that I do think a part of you will hear us through him. Oh my. It's hard to say goodbye, so I'll say see you soon and you be looking for us, ok?

Lynch

6 p.m.

Several visitors have come and gone. The nurse Valerie came. She is wonderful. The catheter was put in and that should help.

Mama is so weak.

7:30 p.m.

Mama was hurting so bad. It's my fault. I wanted to have nothing to do with the meds. I was scared that I would push too much. I was wrong and I will stick with what I'm sure Mama is feeling. I'm so sorry. I was wrong. Jane is giving her water when it kicked in so hard. I should have been sitting with her. Mama became very agitated as the meds started to take affect. She said, "I'm so weak" "I don't want to be weak", then "I don't want to not ready to die. Does too much talk disrupt her thoughts as she works out the beginning of her journey?

9 p.m.

We gave her the meds. Trina has been sitting and giving her water. Darwin is here. Trina asked for us all to pray. Trina, myself, Jane, Brad, and Daddy gave our words to God. Darwin was giving Mama some souse. He is giving her water with a sponge.

5-23 7 a.m.

Mama had a good night. She slept and the meds this morning were stretched. Maybe it has been the stimulation. I don't know. Trina said they got Daddy up and he sat with her. He is still here, his hand next to her arm. As he reads, Adam and Trina again sat up with Mama. Adam was cooking a big breakfast when I woke. Over the past days there has been so many come and go. The stories flow. There are many hugs, kisses, tears, and laughter. Good meals, admiration or Mama's garden and home. A desire to hold Mama's hand and hug her. A need to hear her say hello and I love you. What is so wonderful is that all of these thoughts and desires of each individual over these past days are typical of what all have always thought and felt towards Mama and Daddy. It's not that she is dying. All that we see has always, from my earliest memories, had a place in Mama and Daddy's home. That is beautiful.

9:30 a.m.

Yesterday I was so tired. After Valerie left I thought do and are people thinking that I've pushed the pain meds too much. I know that's ridiculous. I've such a hard time separating memories that are fearful of Trinie. Like Adam and Trina have said "we don't know" I fear pain, Adam starvation, Trina, Mama's inability to think and process. We all have our fears. We all are tired physically and more so emotionally.

10:30 a.m.

Adam and Angie have been with Mama we had to give Mama a suppository. Adam got up to help as he does. Trina is back with Pearson. This is so foreign yes natural to us all and I can't imagine now this is for the grandchildren. Mama is relaxed. Angie is lightly toughing her hair. Her only thoughts are "Bubbas" how many times has she said her name for Daddy? The other is "precious".

Anna has driven all the way out to Leipers Fork for yoga class. I'm proud of my dear children. It is a long drive for her. Jesse has cleaned the kitchen and helped Sally.

About Lori. She has gone for the medicine each time. This may seem like a small thing but it is a sacrifice because no one wants to leave. She's worked so well with the children. As Daddy said "she's a go getter".

We've shut off a door to the kitchen and Trina has ordered "Quiet". She is right. Daddy is cutting off visits. Most communication as we desire is done. I think that now the true waiting begins. The tears will continue but they will be fed from a different source. I wonder if Mama can dream? I hope so. Regardless of her saying I don't want to die a few days ago I can say Mama did not have fear of the act or questions of the after life. We would have seen constant distress had that been the case. The reason for wanting to continue was and has always been for "Bubbas" and "Precious babies".

10 p.m.

Mama is asleep. Daddy is asleep in a chair next to Mama. He doesn't want to go to bed. Maybe he figures the time is very near. All were here and all gone except Trina, Sara,

Angie, Lori H., Adam, Brad and myself. Pat and Darwin took all to the Terminator. Mama was saying words and one sentence. She asked for Bubbas. When Darwin came with his family he opened the door and Mama said "Bubbas" and I said "no Mama that's Darwin". And Mama said "Darwin". It was so nice. Her littlest son who has only made her laugh and be proud.

Trina got Daddy to go to bed. He shook his head no for me. He is so tired. I know how we all feel now drained. All are physically and emotionally drained. I find myself angry that God does not take my Mama. I pray that this will happen.

We've given Mama another suppository so she will sleep. Trina does not think it will be tonight and I agree. I hope we are both wrong.

Today I had 3 neighbors call. Mrs. Ryan across the road gave a strawberry cake. Ann and Nelson came and Bobby Johnson and wife Mr. Johnson will do the service. He is one of 3 couples in the core. The "herd" Daddy calls them. Mr. Johnson's wife was a friend of Mrs. Brazil's and Daddy's early on in college. The herd consists of the Brazils, the Johnsons, and the Boones. It's all too hard to imagine.

Sara

10:53 p.m.

Brad had a great idea. Tomorrow we will put Jackie's glasses on so she may be able to see her pretty flowers Adam has been bringing in each day from her garden.

Right now, Adam is giving her a dose of pain medicine and a sip of Dr. Pepper. He is dropping it in her mouth with a straw. Sally is watching from the door, and turned to go back to the kitchen. Instinctively, she knows something isn't right with her best friend. Darwin and Lori brought their children this evening and Jackie responded as much as I've seen all day. She loves them so much and all of her grandchildren. Lynch has told me that she continued the chemo treatments long enough for Darwin's children to have a memory of her. He has the youngest of the grandchildren. She tolerated it as long as she could but it made her so sick. I really think she was in more pain than any of us knew. But she made use of that time to build memories in the hearts and minds of her grandchildren. We all went to Pickett in November just 6 months ago.

Lynch

5-24-09 11 a.m.

The time is close. Lee Ann the nurse said less than 24 hours probably before 8 p.m. Many many tears. For me this is the first number. Trina is sitting with Mama speaking with her. Mama makes noises. I cried and cried holding Mama's hand on my head in the way she would comfort me and through it all it all she still comforted me with a weak and full of love "don't cry".

Everyone has been called. Jane is on her way. Brad and Darwin soon. Mama, Daddy, Trina, Angie, Sara, Lealand, Adam, and myself are here. As Sara said Mama will sing her alto in Heaven on this day of worship. I assured Mama that we would take care of Daddy and each other and that we would raise our children in the right way so that we all will be together in Heaven. Trina is getting Daddy. I'll leave as we generally do.

Brad and Darwin are here. Larry from Pickett called. Daddy is here. Mama is so very weak. Her breathing slow and her strong heart ready to rest. God is ready and so very soon Mama will leave her body. She will always be with us. I know such things are always said but Mama and Daddy are different. Out people have done so many things. Something strong and unique is in us.

3:35 p.m.

We've given Mama her suppository and pain meds. Anna helped me hold Mama. I'm so proud of her. Before we gave her the meds Nelson and Ann visited. Nelson took Pearson out to see his pistol. Later she told me of Trinie taking shotgun slugs and killing 7 deer in one year. Trina is looking at Mama. It's Trinie. I remember it so well. Daddy, Trina, Darwin, and I are here sitting. Adam is resting. Adam took the bulk of each night on himself.

Mama is almost there.

The girls tell of Mama taking them skinny dipping late one night at Trinie and Dandy's. She cooked the best fried chicken. It was my favorite growing up. Mama took the fried pieced that fell off and set it to the side. Soaked in grease and so good. The best was our birthdays. She made the best. So many nights we would lie on the couch and get our backs rubbed and scratched by Mama. Mama and Daddy gave us so much freedom because they had faith in us. There's no doubt that we were wild. Mama used, generally, a black English riding crop on us. Mark and Mel Burton spent summer after summer with us. It's amazing. People were in and out always.

I wish it would end on this second. We all wait for our lives to change. What gives our family strength is that we have never allowed the history of our people to die. They were by and large extraordinary people. Like Mama would say, "Remember who you are". We are a family of story tellers. Mama will be told in stories beyond all who are now in this house.

Sara

Sunday, late afternoon

The girl that used to baby-sit for your children out in the country just came by. She brought a huge picnic basket full of breads, tea, coffee, fresh rosemary, and an assortment of other things. It looked like something you would have put together, so beautifully displayed, I didn't want to unpack it all. And a big bouquet of fresh pink roses. I could tell she loves you so much and had fond memories.

It's Sunday, Jackie, when will you take your journey? When will you be in that heavenly home I can only attempt to conceptualize in my human mind. My mother sings soprano, so you'll make good harmony together with your alto voice. You've been on many great trips and adventures in your life time-from the Amazon to Wales, but you are about to go on the best journey ever. And Jesus has purchased the ticket with his blood. A one way ticket for all of us; imagine that. We'll have the best family all together we've ever had before too long. And we will get to stay forever. (That's always the worst part of our trips to Pickett and the girl trip to Estil-on the last day, we had to pack up and go home.) We won't have to pack up and go home because we will be home.

Lynch

5 or 6 p.m.

Mary and Johnny Dunlap came by. It was nice to see them. Mary loved Mama so. Leah, Lillie, and Anna have been watching Mama. It appears as though all is the same. Possibly her pulse has slowed? Who knows. Most all are here except the little ones. Brad and

Darwin will stay the night. We will all be here. All of Mama's "precious babies". The neighbors from just down the road came by. They own the dog that Sally plays with every morning. The lady plays the cello for Nash S.O. and wrote a beautiful song and allowed Mama to have a copy that is as yet published. You see people such as this as well as many many others gravitate towards Mama and Daddy. Daddy has very specific ideas for the Memorial Service. He wants a table full of things that Mama made. Dolls, dresses, earrings, maybe pictures of the house, garden, my brothers, and sister. I'm proud of the girls. They have all handled themselves in such a mature manner. This has been difficult. To watch someone you love so dearly is tough. The experience of seeing that this is what on does could effect decades of people of our line. Such good girls. All have stepped up for a person they love. Leah, Lillie, Anna, Jesse, and Lealand. They were more than just adults. Much more.

   7:30 p.m.

We are all here. Daddy, Brad, Trina, Darwin, Adam and myself. Daddy said "Bubbas is here beside you", and Mama made a loud noise. No "Bubbas" this time, but she is aware. I can say Mama never gave up. Family problems, physical, it didn't matter. She moved ahead.

Sara

   5-25-09 2:30 a.m.

I want to be sitting next to Jackie to savor the last moments I have with her. She's been so good to me. I look at her hands and think of all the wonderful things she's done with them. She's held my husband's hand as an infant and changed his diapers. She fed him. Those hands sewed me and Easter outfit when I didn't have money to buy one. It was min green-a skirt and matching top. She took my measurements and her fingers lovingly touched me. Lone before that, she sewed my going away dress after the wedding. It was whit with a green silk belt. I was so proud to wear that-I felt beautiful because she had picked out the fabric and pattern. And my maternity clothes were sewn by those hands. The same hands that drove me to the hospital and held my first child soon after she was born. Those hands wrote many loving notes and stuck a little something in them every year on my birthday. They scrubbed and cleaned many meals. All you've done with our hands and they are still soft and beautiful. Anna has your pinky finger. Lynch laughed at me when I pointed that out after she was born, but now she sees it too. Jesse has your hair. You know, if it weren't for you, I wouldn't have my husband or my daughters. Not just who they are as a branch of your family tree, but what they've become through your wit and wisdom, your example. And now that I look back on my life I wouldn't be all that I am if you had not encouraged me and taught me to be courageous. I think my mother must have prayed very earnestly for me to find the right husband. It hasn't been easy, but you helped me through with all that straight forward advice. You were sent to me to help me become the person I am. Someone to take up where my mother left off. I make a lot of mistakes and bad choices, but I've learned that I don't have to be perfect. Thanks for teaching me that. So, all that you taught me about strength and courage, I'll need when you're gone.

It is the early dawn of Jesse's 14th birthday and I'm remembering how you and George drove back out to South Dakota to help us move when we came back to Nashville. Today she is the age I was when my mother died. But she has had a stronger support system in place as she sees you go. My girls are learning these past few days how to let go and realize that God is in control. His timing is always perfect.

Lynch

4:00 a.m.

Trina woke Daddy. I woke and got up then was told. I've gotten up the others. We are close. Breathing is as described. Thank God my Mama's time in this body is near its end/ Soon very soon. All of us are here. There is some light early dawn. Daddy sits here. Trina stood across the bed. Darwin and I behind Daddy. Brad in Daddy's chair. Adam next to the door in the small chair. I called Jane and gave Mama a kiss for her. Daddy kisses her on the forehead. He has whispered to Mama, "It's over". Lori Hamilton is back and sits by the door. Darwin is on the phone with the nurses and Sara now sits next to me. Daddy's left hand rests on Mama's shoulder. She's left. I don't know what time it is. It's about 6:30 a.m. and Daddy just said he'd call it 5:22 a.m. 5-25-09. I'll write no more in this.

Baba Memories from the Cousins

(started by Lillie and typed by Jesse)

Lillie

When I was little, Baba would always fix me peanut butter crackers, potato chips from the goose tin, and chocolate (monkey) milk for lunch.

One time, Baba told me that "butthole" was her new favorite word.

One day when Papa picked me and Pearson up from school, we came to their house to find Baba standing on the dining room table to fix the chandelier ornaments.

One night at Estill, me and Baba stayed up till midnight watching Hulk Hogan on the show "Hogan Knows Best".

After school, me and Baba always watch Oprah and Rachel Ray.

When we were at Green Hills Grill, Baba told the waiter that he better not spit in our drinks or she would scare him with her eye.

Baba never gets embarrassed if I accidentally walk in on her peeing.

When I was little and would take naps at Baba's, she always set up the rail on the bed so I wouldn't roll off in my sleep.

When Mama and Daddy went to NY, me and Baba and Pearson went to Estill for a week. She scratched my back when I was sad and missed my parents.

Baba's back scratches are the best.

One time, Baba got a "taste" for the old Birthday cake she always makes. The one with white icing and chocolate cake. I learned how to make it and helped spread the icing.

Baba's Dr. Pepper cup never leaves her side. It always has a lipstick ring around the straw.

Before Baba learned how to pay her bills online, she always did them on the desk in the corner of their living room.

Baba loves to play Solitare on the computer.

Shane used to try to say "Grandma", but it always came out "Go-ba". When Leah tried to say "Go-ba" it came out "Baba". That is why we call her Baba.

Baba bought me a blue sequin purse on a shopping trip. It's from "My Friend's Place" in Green Hills.

One time Baba bought me an orange sweater from Anthropology.

Baba always has cut outs from catalogs sitting on the counter.
Me and Baba always go to the flea market together.

Baba makes the best cobbler.

Baba hates when people steal her pears from the pear tree in Estill.

Me, Baba, and Mama like to go fabric shopping.

Baba was once on a TV show for her garden. Baba let me stay upstairs at their house when the 7th Harry Potter book came out.

One time Baba said that I looked red as a lobster when I came out of the bath.

Baba set up pee mats around the corners of their house when Huey got old.

Baba loves going to the dog park with Sally.

One time I gained seven pounds by going to Estill with Baba.

Baba took me and Anna to Sonic in Estill, a lot, late at night.

Baba hates the commercial with the whiney kid that said "more cake please".

One time, when I was only about eleven, Baba said that she could talk about anything in front of me because I was practically an adult.

Baba has a pan for a castle cake.

Baba makes the most delicious rolls.

When Baba had long hair, she wore scrunchies.

I always wake up with Baba at Estill to go sit on the porch to watch the humming birds and the ants bump into each other.

Any of my friends who have met Baba, immediately love her.

Baba is the coolest grandma in her black pick up truck.

When we were little Baba always filled her truck up with water so we could play in it.

It was Baba's idea to hide the frog everytime we went to Estill.

Baba loves to work in her garden.

Baba is sometimes annoyed by Paula Dean.

Me, Baba, Papa, and Leah went to Cammo Peal in Estill for Mexican food and got a table that was infested with flies.

I always help Baba when she has trouble with her ipod.

Baba loves taking pictures, and one time she took a photography class.

Baba calls Papa Bubbas and he calls her Babes. They are madly in love.

Baba used to workout at Curves.

Baba loves the feeling of Sally's stomach and ears. She likes how Sally's tongue can lick in between her toes.

I'll never forget looking into Baba's eye and holding her soft hand when she whispered "I'm proud of you" to me.

Baba sewed long pouch things for people to put their plastic bags in. It has a convenient hole in the bottom.

One time, while all the cousins were sitting at a table in Estill eating, Baba said that she noticed how all her grandchildren had beautiful lips.

Baba loved to play chicken foot.

One time, while playing chicken foot, Baba meant to say "your turn Jesse," but her words jumbled together and she said "jerk" to Jesse. We all were laughing forever because Baba had called Jesse a jerk.

Baba loves horses.

Baba thinks that the tree in her garden looks like a dancer.

Me and Lealand used to ride in the little red and yellow car at Baba's house.

Mama and Daddy's wedding was at Baba's house. Baba cussed at the flower man.

One time Baba said "damn" because the mammogram was squeezing her boobies and it hurt.

Baba sewed me a light pink skirt with hot pink and polka dot ribbons on it.

Baba gave me her ostridge feather hat.

Baba gave me the rainbow mats that are in my room.

Baba has applesauce with every dinner, no matter what else she is having.

When we got lost on the island Baba thought that everyone was over acting. When we were being lectured she said "We have an Easter egg hunt. Now, lets go have some fun!"

Baba's milk always gets a little frozen and has ice in it.

Me and Baba's widgys always hurt when we are on high places.

Baba likes people to pull a whole bunch of grapes off and not just one at a time because she thinks it's ugly that way.

Baba loved her book about Hiroshima and one time we sat at the kitchen table and she told me the whole story.

Baba always bought a big box of assorted chips for Estill.

One of my favorite meals that Baba fixed was at Estill. It was tilapia and creamed corn.

Baba always said "Come Sally...Come, come" and she blew a whistle at her.

Whenever anyone goes into Baba's house we call "Yoo hoo" and Baba says "Yoo hoo" back.

Baba says febreeze like "fa-breeze".

Baba loves to eat combos when she's in Estill.

Baba likes to listen to books on her ipod.

Me, Mama, and Baba went into Buckle in the Coolsprings Mall and Baba found me a cute shirt.

I love when Baba plays with my hair.

Baba always has the freezer in Estill in the laundry room stocked with ice pops.

Baba always keeps a wooden block taped to the toy chest in the living room so little fingers won't get smashed when it closes.

Baba used to tell me that she was a tap dancer in a lot of her dreams.

I have a long torso and short legs just like Baba.

One time when me and Mama went to Radner we brought Baba some tiny wildflowers. When we brought them to her, she had a perfect tiny little vase for them and put them in the windowsill.

Baba told Pearson that she would pay him to get in trouble at school, just to see what would happen.

Baba always lovingly made fun of Papa for biting the hair off his knuckles.

For a special dinner Baba would heat us up some pizza rolls (and of course applesauce).

Baba always fixes the corners of rugs when they are folded up.

Baba always liked the idea of me marrying a black man. She thinks white and black babies are so pretty.

Baba always has opera music playing when you walk into the house.

I remember sitting on the porch at Estill trying to teach Baba to text.

Baba texted me one time to tell me a story about Papa spraying a hose at the bats in Estill.

Baba wanted us to paint the water heater in Estill like a whale.

One time when we all went on a walk. I put my hand on Baba's bottom and said "Baba I'm touching your bottom".

Anna

Me and Lillie used to play with Baba's arm fat, and we named it Bob.

All the cousins used to come over to Baba's house every single day.

She would always bring out the little pool for us to swim in.

One time at Pickett, Baba drove us to the beach in her truck and the rain felt like needles all over.

Baba was brushing my hair one time and told me her hair was so long when she was little and it hurt when her mom brushed it.

Me, Lillie, and Jesse gave Baba a makeover at Estill and she sang opera to us.

Baba ALWAYS sits on the right side of the couch.

When Baba came to Grandparents' Day I was always so excited.

Baba taught me to play Solitare.

One year Baba got me and Leah some baggy black pants with chains because she thought they were cute.

I used to love getting in Baba's bed and talking to her with Hewie in the morning.

When Baba had surgery she said she had lost her social filter. She was afraid she would say something inappropriate.

Sometimes Baba didn't wear a bra. She didn't care though.

Me and Lillie and Baba tried to drag the giant float at Estill into the sun. It was so hard.

Baba watched the Dog Whisperer to learn how to train Sally.

Me and Jesse went shopping for doorknobs for Estill. We were there for like an hour and we didn't even buy anything. (with Baba)

I also went to pick out Estill furniture with her.

My middle name (Jacquelyn) is Baba's name. They spell it differently though.

Baba and all of the cousins used to smuggle food into the movies.

Baba took us to see Ever After in the movie theatres.

Baba said Trini told people to wear a life jacket to bed if they slept on the porch at Estill. Just in case it fell in the lake.

Baba got mad at Papa because he almost parked in a handy capped spot.

Baba's fingers have always been crooked.

Leah

Baba said the filter between her brain and her mouth was gone after surgery, but I think she just thought it was a funny excuse to say inappropriate things.

Baba let us have a flour fight when she taught us how to make rolls.

Baba bought me a skull t-shirt and baggy black pants.

Baba always let us ride in the back of her pick up truck at Pickett. One time it started pouring rain while all the grankids were in the back. Construction workers laughed at us.

She wore purple Ugg boots.

Baba always makes lists of things she wants to get done.

Sally loves to sit on the couch with Baba.

I loved to try on Baba's dresses. I thought they were so beautiful! But, in the middle school I outgrew the dresses. She had such a tiny ribcage!

There's always a tin full of cookies at Baba's house, but she gets annoyed when people eat too many.

At the movies, Baba and Papa can balance a bag of popcorn between their knees.

Baba bought me a purse that looked like a Chinese takeout container. It had a lime green fabric and an orange handle.

Mama wanted Baba to discourage me from getting a tattoo, but Baba just said she had always wanted one.

For graduation, Baba bought me one emerald earring for my cartilage piercing. I haven't taken it out since I got it.

I have the name Katrine, just like Trini, Baba, and my Mama. I'm so proud of that, and I tell everyone.

I also tell everyone she made a boy cry when she out-shot him.

Jesse

Baba once let me help her prepare shrimp. She laughed when I told her I liked the tails.

Once we had a "slug race". Baba got mad when she asked us to clean up a mess, and we said, "slug races last a long time".

When I fell off the horse at Pickett, I forgot the word for "hyperventilate" and said "I was hallucinating!" to Baba. She got scared.

Baba went to see Benjamin Button with us. When it started everyone was quite. Right then she asked Trina, "Did you taste that Broccoli Soup? It was sooo good!" really loud.

When we went to the Rainforest Café, I road with Baba because I felt bad for her. Everyone else was riding with Trina.

Baba drove us through NEEDLE rain at Pickett. We only had one towel to cover like nine cousins. People we drove past laughed and I always felt like Baba was laughing along with them.

The washing machine says her name at Estill.

Baba never yelled. She laughed and said something sarcastic.

Whenever I see something crazy looking with my mom, I say "That's like what Baba would wear."

Baba gave the girls pretty heart pendants one Christmas.

When I peed in the computer room it changed the color of the floor in between the tile. She didn't care. She just cleaned it up.

Baba didn't mind when we would hang out in her closet.

Baba didn't mind when we went skinny dipping at Estill. Actually, I think she supported it, as something fun.

At Estill, I tripped on a rusty nail. She put medicine and a Dora Explorer band aide.

Baba used to let us spin on the octagon shaped table. Until someone would fall off.

I always stared at her neck flab. If she caught me, she'd jiggle it.

Pearson

I liked when I was playing basket ball and the clock was going out and we were about to lose and my coach told me to hold the ball and wait until the game was over and Baba screamed SHOOT IT and I looked at her and shook my head no.

And I liked it when Baba shot my 22 rifle.

I told my mom Baba is not like all those other prissy grandmothers who just stay inside and cook and sits around all day but Baba is an out door woman who shoots a big old 12 gage. I love Baba.

Izzy

Baba and I made a yummy fruit cake together that was for a Christmas party.

When I came over for a sleepover, we made an outfit. It was a pink skirt with white lace and a tube top with lace straps.

She loved Sudoku, and she introduced it to me, and now I love it.

Whenever I came over to hang out, she would tickle and scratch me.

She always made me chocolate milk. The "monkey kind!"

I always admired her taste her taste in clothes, she had a funky edge to everything she wore.

For my 11th b-day she gave me one of Trini's bracelets. She said she would give it to me because she knew that I would treasure it and take care of it.

She would always let me jiggle her arm flab. She would never get embarrassed, either.

When I went for a sleep over, we watched a movie together and we both shed tears.

She loved FLUFFO. It was a treat that she enjoyed!

She always acted like a proper lady, no matter what she looked or felt like.

She didn't care if 20 people were at her house at the same time. She actually enjoyed it.

At Estill, we always skinny dipped. (and some people peed!!!!)

Baba would always have chips, cookies, and Diet Dr. Pepper stocked in her house.

My favorite thing she made for me was her chocolate banana pudding. Since I loved it so much, she made it my special desert!

I was sooo excited when Baba gave me some of her eye shadow.

Baba would always write down funny things we said.

She would always put our school pictures up on the wall by the light switch.

Baba hated the old dishwasher, and wanted a new one.

Creed

I loved how the dryer at Estill said Baba.

Also she would scratch my back real good.

She could always make a funny joke up.

She dressed in the coolest clothes ever.

It was fun when Baba floored it when were coming home from Estill.

I always went over to Baba's and had a great time.

There was nothing boring about her.

She was always a better shot then Annie Oakley!

Zoe

She liked to point her crooked finger at people.

Baba let me and India sit in her bathroom sink and play in the water.

Baba always drank Slim Fast for lunch.

Baba did flips with us into our pool.

Baba's clothes always matched her jewelry.

Baba let us use her lip stick.

Baba had cool glasses.

Baba made good cobbler with fruit.

Baba always scratched my back while we watched TV.

I jiggled her arm flab.

Her washer said Ba-Ba, Ba, Ba.

I loved it when she came to Grandparent's Day.

For my B-Day she made me a money flower.

She always picked cards that had something I liked.

She made me chocolate milk with the bunny on the front.

She swang me on the swing set and she
~~always~~
always sang and song that came From ~~it~~
her ~~beautiful~~ voes.
beautiful

India & Zeke

*She let me play in her sink.

She put lipstick on me.

She played with me.

She loves me. She likes me. She cares about me.

She let me draw.

She was a nice grandma.

She let me eat Cheez-its and cookies.

*I love Baba and I hug her and I love to go to her house, be with her, and see her and I want her to be happy in heaven with God.

Lealand & Livia

*My favorite thing about her was that she did not judge people. I had a friend who recently met Baba and many people would have thought he was a little sketchy because of the way he dressed, but when he left Baba said, "Well he seemed like a nice boy."

*Baba was the best back scratcher.

My Mother   8-20-2016

When you died and everyone else wrote something about you, I never did. I didn't know if anyone noticed, but for some reason, I wouldn't make myself do it. Now that Daddy is doing this book, I feel that I should. It also seems that it should be less hard. I can't possibly write down everything that I could, because most of it is feeling. I will write what comes to me — things that only I know, that you knew, things that will always be with me in my heart, in my soul.

- I remember being a little girl and you were my beautiful mother. When you and Daddy went out you would put make up on in your bathroom. You had a stool, you sat on and would open a drawer on the left side of your vanity. I would close the top of the toilet and sit on it and watch you. I never asked to put on makeup and I don't remember wanting to. I remember your eyelash curler.

- Back then your jewelry was in the dresser with the large mirror. You would let me look at it. You always kept each piece in the small box that it came in. You let me look at the old special pieces that belonged to grandmothers. I always was careful and I always put it away.

- I didn't like it when you would go to "town". That is what we said when you went to Nashville. When you went to Franklin, we said you are going to Franklin. You were gone longer when you went to town, but you would bring me something little, but it seemed so special. My favorite thing was a package of tiny chicklets. It seemed so, so special for some reason.

- I remember your black hair. I remember you letting me play with it and brush it. I felt like you "let" me, like it was special, but I am sure it felt really good to you.

- I always wanted you to scratch my back. I loved having my head in your lap. There was no better place to be. We all wanted that I'm sure.

- You made us feel safe.

- I don't remember you being silly when I was little, but I grew to know you as silly. You loved thinking that you were funny. You were funny, but the funniest part was that you really "thought" you were funny & you sort of were.

" I loved that about you and you knew it.

- I remember you in the kitchen. You cooked, & cooked & cooked. You fed us well. We had desserts maybe a lot when we were little.

- I remember being with you in your garden in front of the house. It was so hot but you made a little place for me to sit. I think that I had a thermos of water.

- I remember going to the fair. You would take a damp washcloth in a baggie to wipe our mouths & hands. (no wipes back then)

- I remember you dressing me to play in the snow. Layers & layers of clothes & socks. Baggies on the feet to make slipping our foot in the boots easier. That is what I thought anyway. Was it an additional attempt to keep our feet dry? I don't know. You would cake chapstick on our cheeks to keep them from chaping.

- You let us roam & roam. Even me. Did you ever worry? You didn't seem to.

- You sewed and sewed. When we would go shopping for me — you would always say . . .

"I can make that". Now, I know what you made me was cuter than what we could buy, but I remember wanting a store bought dress.

- you made all of my nice dresses. You always were creative. You could figure out the demensions, design, do the math on any curtain, dress, etc.

- You said that you weren't artistic, but you were so creative. You had great vision, ideas & could execute anything in your head.

- You had a Billy Jack hat! an afro wig a fall (wig), a ~~this~~ braided hair head band.

- you had a big truck, electric blue, side pipes & an air horn on the top. I was in Jr. high & it embarrassed me.

- Everyone loved you

- You spanked with your hand

- You told me that the only regret that you had in your life was not trying out for Cyprus Gardens. Your parents discouraged it. You didn't like that.

- You didn't brag about yourself

- If we said "yes" to you when we wer young you would say "yes what"

- You would call me in the morning and tell me all of the things that you had been thinking about the night before if you couldn't sleep.

- You once told me that I was your best friend. I remember acting normal about it, but I was shocked that you said that because I didn't know that you felt that way. You were always my mother, a parent, when you said that, it was the greatest honor of my life. I never tell those things because that is between us.

- When you were sick, you once said to me that you wanted me to be with you at the doctor's office because I knew how you thought. You said, "you know how I think". I knew that I did, but I didn't know that you knew that too. That was another joy and honor to me.

- I hated when I couldn't talk to you. I knew you were tired, but I missed when I couldn't talk to you all the time. I never told you that because I knew that you would worry about me.

- When you cooked, you knew how the things were to be eaten, if things were meant to be eaten in a certain order b/c of what they were, You always wanted to make sure we understood that.

- When I was pregnant w/ Leah you went to the ultra sound you saw Leah's big eyes and you just loved it.

- You saw Leah being born. You had 5 children & never saw a baby being born. You loved it.

- You drove me to the hospital when I had Lillie b/c of Pat's feet. She came so fast. You were worried about me.

- I nursed my babies & I knew that you wished you had nursed yours but they didn't encourage that when you had babies.

- I remember you sterilizing baby bottles. Washing cloth diapers for Adam & Darwin.

- When I was a young mother — you never made me feel like I didn't know what I was doing. You always said the perfect thing. You loved your grandchildren. I am so happy they knew you. No grand child ever had a better grandmother.

- I loved going to Estill with you. You always made it special. I loved sleeping in the bed with you.

- You were naughty. When we got older + you didn't have to be so parental all the time that is when I knew you were silly. You wanted to shoot birds (w/ your middle finger) you told Lillie you liked to say butt hole

- You loved Daddy but you loved to laugh at him

- You loved Sally

- you once punched a pony in the nose

- you wore a bikini when you were a little bit too old. I never told you that I thought that

- you loved your mother. I wondered how you could stand to not have her. I know how - she was in you and you had me. It is the same with me.

-I loved going to Mexico with you. You took me. That made me feel so special. I know that you wanted me to have a good life.

-You didn't tell me about a test you were having when I went to Peru b/c you didn't want me to worry + not go. I was annoyed. I now realize that you worried about me more than you let me know + I worried about you more than I let you know.

- We both knew that we were being brave.

- There are a million things I could say, a million pages to write and I couldn't say enough.

When you died, I had a dream about you. I knew you were dead but it was o.k. I was communing with you. You didn't talk, but you told me that "Everything is ok" you didn't say will be. I understood what you meant.

I think about you, but not really. I feel about you. That is why I didn't want to write – thinking about you hurts. Feeling about you doesn't. That is why we didn't always say things that it seems like we would have. I know you knew. I love you

153

To our grandchildren –

Be courteous and kind to others and expect them to treat you the same. Do not tolerate rudeness or mean spiritedness.

Stay close to your family and friends and help them when thy need it.

Do your best to be honest and forgiving.

Always keep reading and learning.

Stand up for the poor, the weak and the underdogs. Jesus is a good example to follow.

Never get pompous or arrogant.

Take care of your health and have fun – lots of it.

Don't waste your time, and that of others, complaining and being negative; that's boring and tiring. Have a positive purpose to your life – it can help give you peace.

Enjoy your work or do something else.

Fight against bigotry and injustice. Fight for that which is good and right. Never give in!

Get to know people who are really different from you and learn from them.

If you marry, take good care of your spouse and, if you fail, beg for forgiveness and change your ways.

Enjoy nature, art, good literature, music, and things that are beautiful,

"Baba" and I love you, George "Papa" Spain, June 2016

P.S.— Have a lot of fun! Break the bone of life open and suck all the marrow out!

Jackie

I'll See You Soon

George

Ideas into Books®
W E S T V I E W
P.O. Box 605
Kingston Springs, TN 37082
www.publishedbywestview.com

ISBN 978-1-62880-116-3

First edition, Christmas 2016

Printed in the United States of America on acid free paper.

www.ingramcontent.com/pod-product-compliance
Lightning Source LLC
Chambersburg PA
CBHW042030090426

42811CB00016B/1801